Classroom
Communit

This book presents the practice and vision of classrooms that operate as learning communities.

In classrooms that operate as learning communities, the social and learning purposes advance together through all participants being involved and engaged in building knowledge. This is a new way of seeing and managing classrooms and offers:

- an integration of what's best in learning and what's best in the social life of classrooms;
- a vision of the role of the teacher that is more creative and more related to the commitment of teachers;
- a more connected view of school, in contrast to the mechanistic view that currently dominates;
- an answer to the short-term performance pressure of politicians – better performance, better behaviour, better social development.

After reading *Classrooms as Learning Communities* any classroom teacher will feel more able to take steps towards building a more effective classroom with the aspects of learning communities they choose.

Chris Watkins is Reader in Education at the Institute of Education, University of London.

What's in it for schools?

Edited by Kate Myers and John MacBeath

The *What's in it for Schools?* series aims to make educational policy issues relevant to practitioners. Each book in the series focuses on a major educational issue. The authors set the issues in context, look at how it impacts on the daily lives of schools and teachers, and raise key questions. The books are grounded in solid theory, recent research evidence and best practice, and will make an excellent addition to any staffroom bookshelf.

Inspection: What's in it for schools?
James Learmonth

Leadership: What's in it for schools?
Thomas J. Sergiovanni

School Improvement: What's in it for schools?
Alma Harris

Assessment: What's in it for schools?
Paul Weeden, Jan Winter and Patricia Broadfoot

It's About Learning (and It's About Time)
Louise Stoll, Dean Fink and Lorna Earl

Consulting Pupils: What's in it for schools?
Julia Flutter and Jean Rudduck

Classrooms as Learning Communities: What's in it for schools?
Chris Watkins

Classrooms as Learning Communities
What's in it for schools?

Chris Watkins

Routledge
Taylor & Francis Group

LONDON AND NEW YORK

First published 2005
by Routledge
2 Park Square, Milton Park, Abingdon, Oxon OX14 4RN

Simultaneously published in the USA and Canada
by Routledge
270 Madison Ave, New York, NY 10016

Routledge is an imprint of the Taylor & Francis Group

© 2005 Chris Watkins

Typeset in Baskerville
by Keystroke, Jacaranda Lodge, Wolverhampton
Printed and bound in Great Britain
by TJ International Ltd, Padstow, Cornwall

British Library Cataloguing in Publication Data
A catalogue record for this book is available from the British Library

Library of Congress Cataloging in Publication Data
A catalog record for this book has been requested

ISBN 0–415–32779–2 (Hbk)
ISBN 0–415–32780–6 (Pbk)

Contents

List of figures

List of tables

Preface

During the final stages of the preparation of this book, I was visiting a school in Acton in order to develop a learning project with staff. Four 14-year-old pupils were given the task of showing me around the school, and I soon explained a little about my interest.

We settled in the corner of a playground, and I asked, 'In the four years that you've been at this school, what has been your best learning experience?'

Two of them immediately flashed a glance of recognition at each other and started to talk about a class they were in:

'The teacher was really interested in the subject.'
'She really cared for kids.'
'*It was just like a mini community.*'

As my mouth hung open with amazement at this summary description, I dared to think that pupils, as well as the many teachers I have worked with, might welcome what this book is trying to do.

Acknowledgements

The idea that this is my first 'single-authored' book in fifteen years is a peculiar fiction. Our achievements are never exclusively our own. Many people have contributed, sometimes in ways that they do not know. Their voices will be found within these pages.

I am privileged to work with many people on aspects of learning, and will leave many out as I honour those with whom I have been working most directly on the themes of this book in recent years. They include my closest teaching colleagues at the Institute of Education, University of London: Eileen Carnell, Caroline Lodge, Jane Reed and Eleanore Hargreaves.

And they include very many teachers I am privileged to work and learn with:

Adrian Blake, Ashleigh Arbuthnot, Charlotte Jordan, Claire House, Elisavet Zaroliagki, Emily Callaghan, Emma Skae, Georgios Vlikidis, Grace Churchill, John Craig, Maire McLeish, Naheeda Maharasingam, Nick House, Niketa Vakani, Penny Cox, Peter Shaw, Riaz Rhemtulla, Rose-Marie Hill, Sally Whittle, Yvonne Kurz.

Anne Hayes, Athanasios Liakos, Barrie Murphy, Christian Hicks, Cynthia Wei, Denise Smith, Dorreth Emmerson, Fay Sewell-Hall, Jean-Pierre Le Tissier, Julie Daukes, Kirsten Timbrell, Kostas Sarros, Lisa Hodgkinson, Lucy Wakeman, Mark Williamson, Michelle Smith, Nikoleta Mousiadou, Richard Peers, Shona McIntosh, Steven Denton, Zoe Bonnell.

Alexia Slutzkin, Alyson Stevenson, Andrew Nockton, Anne Pilmoor, Dean Harris, Elaine Kneller, Hayden Burns, Jack Kenny, Jane Webster, John Sullivan, Lindsay Rayner, Louise Miller, Malini Sidhu, Marguerite Chaplin, Norma Gregory, Siân Williams.

Alison Tonkin, Claire Moujaes, Connie Cooling, Eleanor Sykes, Faith Jenkins, Helen Kerslake, Jan Bentley, Jane Roller, Jayne Halliwell, Jess Finer, Juliet English, Kathryn Solly, Lesley Fenton, Liz Thomas, Lynnette Baily, Maggie Futcher, Marion Michaud, Nadia Sultan, Nicky Ostwald, Peppie Saunders, Richard Nicholls, Sarah Goodwyn, Sarah Kearney, Sonia Penfold, Sue Hussey, Tom Goodyer.

Anne Gibbs, Barbara Macintosh, Chris Modi, Dave Fenlan, Dave Wahl, Hilary Belden, Isabel Smith, Jan Lowe, John Parry, Joleene Drage, Marina Abreu, Paula Coulter, Rachel Benjamin, Rebecca Roebuck, Simon Adams, Susan Bird, Terri Murphy, Toni George, Vickie Holland, Zahir Uddin.

And an extra appreciation to Patsy, my co-life-author: now for the holiday!

1   Introduction

Why this book?

This book is intended to support the hopes, visions and practices of classroom teachers, and through that to contribute to creating the classrooms and schools our pupils deserve. In it I aim to communicate three things:

- a vision,
- some of the practices, and
- the evidence

for seeing and promoting classrooms and schools as learning communities. I make that plain at the outset, because it's not particularly common nowadays to be clear and 'up front' about the first element, vision. In much of the literature which finds its way into schools, classrooms are talked about in a way where the vision is not stated. Indeed, there seems to be no need to be clear about vision. This is because such writing rests on a set of unstated assumptions which are prevalent in society and which have become taken for granted in many places. They are a set of mechanical assumptions, and recently they have become commonplace in the official voice and its pronouncements on schools. As Terry Wrigley put it:

> A public discourse has been established which accounts for successful teaching in mechanistic and superficial terms as a set of external behaviours which are not linked to an understanding

of learning. It is based on teacher performance, not interaction between teachers and learners.[1]

This discourse and the prevalent assumptions deserve questioning for two important reasons. First, they may incorporate a limited and limiting set of concerns. For example, many politicians and a minority of anxious parents press their teacher-centred, 'delivery'-centred view of classrooms in response to their short-term performance concerns. The longer-term developmental concerns of individuals and of society are sidelined, and the risks are many. One is that creative and committed teachers become disaffected. As the *Times Educational Supplement* head-line put it: 'Young staff flee factory schools'. Second, the prevalent assumptions may actually be counterproductive for achieving the goals which many stakeholders and the vast majority of educators would hold dear – including the goal of high-level performance! The idea that better performance, even on the many narrow tests which beset pupils nowadays, is achieved through improving the mechanical efficiency of teaching, of routinising our approach to teaching, is challenged by much evidence. By contrast, the evidence is that classrooms which operate as learning communities also get better results.

So I'm writing this book from a stance which includes the belief that current trends towards routinising classrooms are wrong: wrong for pupils, wrong for teachers and wrong for achievement.

The quick-fix instrumental strategies which have been promulgated may be 'more of the same' in terms of the history of classrooms, and as such will not contribute to the transformation which is needed for the times we are in. We need to move from the mechanical and backward-looking 'what works?' to the more human and future-oriented 'what's worth working on?'

This book stands for the idea that it is worth working on the practices which help classrooms to operate as a collective of learners and a learning collective.

Why now?

Recently, the Organisation for Economic Co-operation and Development[2] (OECD) addressed the theme of 'What Schools for the Future?'. Expert papers were invited from people who had given much time to these considerations. They came from the USA, Australia and five European countries (but not the UK). After working on the collected ideas, the report painted a picture of six possible scenarios, two each under three major themes:

The status quo extrapolated
1   Robust bureaucratic school systems;
2   Extending the market model;

The re-schooling scenarios
3   Schools as core social centres;
4   Schools as focused learning organisations;

The de-schooling scenarios
5   Learner networks and the network society;
6   Teacher exodus – the 'meltdown' scenario.

What strikes me about these scenarios is that even in their most limited, single-line descriptions they are recognisable, both to me and to teachers who are introduced to them. The implications which are spelled out at more length in the report are also recognisable:

1   Strong bureaucratic elements and pressures towards uniformity; new tasks and responsibilities continually added to the remit of schools, in the face of the problems in family and community; financial and human resources continually stretched. Despite repeated policy initiatives, the educational inequalities that reflect unequal social and residential home backgrounds/environments prove extremely resilient, as educated parents 'play the system'.
2   Greater privatisation and more mixed public/private partnerships; seriously enhanced risks of inequality and exclusion and of the public school system being relegated to 'residual' status; market approaches cover a bewildering variety of policies.
3   School seen as the most effective bulwark against social fragmentation and a crisis of values; strong sense of schooling as a 'public good'; the individualisation of learning is tempered by

a clear collective emphasis; greater priority is accorded to the social/community role of schools; high levels of public trust.

4   Schools are revitalised around a strong 'knowledge' agenda; academic/artistic/competence development goals are paramount; experimentation and innovation are the norm; innovative forms of assessment and skills recognition flourish; a strong emphasis is placed on educational research and development; ICT is used extensively; the very large majority of schools merit the label 'learning organisations', informed by a strong equity ethos.

5   Quickening abandonment of school institutions through diverse alternatives, stimulated by extensive possibilities via the Internet and powerful and inexpensive ICT; radical de-institutionalisation, even dismantling, of school systems; learning for the young not primarily conferred in particular places called 'school' nor through professionals called 'teachers' nor distinct residential community bases; while promoted as supporting diversity and democracy, also substantial risks of exclusion especially for those students who have traditionally relied on the school as the mechanism for social mobility and inclusion.

6   Teacher recruitment crisis and relative political impotence to address it; education political climate increasingly conflictual; inequalities widen sharply between residential areas, social and cultural groups, etc.; affluent parents in worst-affected areas desert public education in favour of private alternatives; intensive use of ICT as an alternative to teachers; wide disparities possible between highly innovative and traditional uses; solidarity declines and pro-tectionist responses increase, especially if competing for limited pools of qualified staff.

I consider that analysis worth quoting at length because it so clearly describes a range of scenarios, each of which is distinctly possible, and indeed the seeds of many of those scenarios are evident in our schools today.

For me, for the teachers I work with, and for the education profes-sionals canvassed by the OECD, scenarios 3 and 4 are the ones I value and the ones I work to create. The vision of social and learning functions coming together and being served by schools is one which is not only essential for our futures but is also immensely realisable.

What's in it for schools?

Above I have been so bold as to suggest that the very future for schools is in becoming learning communities, and similarly for classrooms within them. Why should schools and teachers be interested in this? Put briefly, because:

1   in learning communities the teachers' role is more focused on learning rather than management, and is more professionally rewarding;
2   in learning communities, pupils develop more competences which are transferable to non-school contexts;
3   learning communities provide a good preparation and a good model for many aspects of a better future life for all.

As a bonus, effective learning communities are associated with better performance, better behaviour, and better social/moral development. More detail on this evidence is to be found in the chapters that follow.

I also feel confirmed that teachers will find much in it for them, for two reasons. The first is that over a number of years, in schools and on courses, I have asked teachers 'what's most important about life in your classroom?'. The replies are many and varied but some patterns also emerge. The teachers I have asked regularly mention:

• the creation of an overall climate in the classroom;
• the social relations between groups of pupils, and how to help them get on;
• the managing of the multiple dimensions of classroom activity.

All these are key considerations in this book. The second reason is that in recent years I have heard from teachers who have experimented with and adapted the sorts of practices this book is about, and hear them talk about inspiring experiences, reclaiming their professional vision, and even relinquishing leadership roles in order to spend more time in the classroom.

Who is the author and whose are the voices?

I have been an educator for over thirty years, and am currently a teacher at the University of London Institute of Education. I come from one of those South Wales families that over-produced teachers all through the last century. Why? To escape the limits of the valleys. So I keep alive a very real vision of expanding learners' horizons. And I honour the sense of community which was found in those valleys, even in times and conditions of adversity. My mother was a primary school teacher for most of her working life.

I have been a maths teacher in a large comprehensive school, a form tutor and a teacher of social education. In all of those contexts I have been especially interested in the personal–social dimensions of learning, classrooms and schools. I have worked with pupils whose effect on schools was sometimes disruptive, have studied on courses in a particularly active approach to school counselling, and have run courses in pastoral care, school behaviour, tutoring, mentoring and so on.

Currently I am course leader to the MA in Effective Learning and have been course leader to an MA in School Development.

As a teacher I currently use most of the classroom practices explored in this book. Indeed, through many of the courses and projects I am currently involved in, the vision and practice has been developed collaboratively with many of the other teachers I am privileged to work and learn with. In my job I intersect with the world of research so am also privileged to examine accounts and evidence from across the world. In both senses of evidence – the lived experience and the research of others – this book is founded in evidence. I value the contribution of research to the practice of teaching, not least on occasions such as when the *TES* said, reviewing my *Managing Classroom Behaviour*: 'Chris Woodhead's comment about never encountering a useful piece of educational research is effectively debunked by this publication'.[3]

The voices of teachers I work and learn with appear in these pages, as do the voices of pupils they work and learn with. They are mentioned in the acknowledgements. But equally important, these pages examine the voices which serve to limit teachers and pupils in their classroom practice and achievement. My understanding of what helps people to achieve their best is that their best goals are often inspiring and moving, yet they can be undermined and disempowered by other voices.

Sometimes these are imagined voices which all of us know – doubt, inertia and, occasionally, fear. But all too often these voices are real – as when the official voice speaks from a view of learning and teaching which is far from inspiring. In order to achieve our best we need to identify those voices, be able to analyse them for what they are, and thereby reduce their life-negating impact.

An outline map of the book

- Chapter 2 considers classrooms and learning, the dominant patterns and the need for change.
- Chapter 3 examines the concept of community as something practical rather than sentimental.
- Chapter 4 reviews research evidence on the outcomes of classrooms as learning communities.
- Then a brief interlude considers how best to consider classroom practices.
- Chapters 5, 6, 7, 8 and 9 look at classroom matters in detail: the goals, tasks, social structure, resources and roles needed.
- Another interlude offers pointers for observing classrooms from this perspective.
- Chapter 10 examines the school context as a wider learning community.

Prompts for reflection

Before you start your journey with that map, try to have in mind your own view of the 'big picture' for schools and their future. Perhaps a question which my friend Guy Claxton asks will help. Do you think that:

(a) schools are doing a good job of preparing most young people for the demands of the future?
(b) they would be, if all the currently mooted reforms were implemented successfully? or
(c) we have got a long way to go?

---

2 Classrooms, change, learning, teaching, community

That's not much of a chapter title is it? But it headlines the issues we need to address in the first section of this book: they are connected issues, and together they forge the framework for the whole enterprise of operating classrooms as learning communities.

Classrooms: the dominant image

Let's face it, if at the beginning of the twenty-first century you were to design an environment for learning, you might not design something which looked and operated like the modal classroom. All across the world, in different cultures, a classroom and its dynamics are easily recognisable and markedly similar. The model which spread throughout the world during the twentieth century, and bears remarkable similarity with the earliest known classrooms of 5,000 years ago, is remarkably dominant and remarkably resilient. It has somehow become 'locked in' as a design, rather like the QWERTY keyboard,[1] long after the reasons for it being that way have passed. If you examine images, prints, paintings and photographs of classrooms over the centuries, you will readily list observable similarities – classroom walls, rows of pupils, status gender and power – but differences are more difficult to identify – occasional changes in technology, and perhaps some reducing social distance between teachers and pupils.

The point of remarking on the resilience of the dominant image of classrooms is not to conclude that nothing can change and to give up on schools! Quite the opposite. We need to recognise and understand the dominant picture in order to better know how to construct something else. And we need to recognise that when making a change from the dominant pattern, it will feel to be more of a change than it really is, just because it goes against the taken-for-granted views which circulate in our society and in us.

How have classrooms managed to stay the same?

Researchers of classroom consistency[2] point to two major sources of stability:

* the characteristics of the classroom situation, and
* the power relations between teachers and pupils.

I would add a third, which reflects the above two but adds another consideration:

* the dominant view of learning and learners.

Let's consider each of these, so that we may understand better the connected changes which occur when teachers build classrooms as learning communities

Classrooms are measurably the most complex social situation on the face of the planet. Teachers may be involved in a thousand or more interactions per day, many of them personally demanding. In this busyness, teachers make decisions fast and they construct routines in order to make classroom life manageable. I remember hearing of a test pilot, who after a placement in schools decided to train as a teacher: when asked to explain, he said that the flying led to an adrenaline rush on each flight, whereas in classroom life it was there all the time. Teachers have precious little time to interact with each individual pupil, so they have to make the classroom operate as a system of activities for groups and learning. At the same time they give considerable mental attention to pupils. Seasoned classroom researchers have given up attempts to categorise teachers' complex considerations about how to respond to individual pupils.

Classrooms are public places. In the classroom, teachers and pupils are highly visible to others. Teachers occasionally feel on stage, and may use audience effects to affect others in the classroom. If the public aspects of the job are emphasised and increased, teachers can react by isolating their performance from view. This explains and may also increase the isolation which sometimes characterises their work. Paradoxically, teachers are psychologically 'alone' in densely populated settings.

Classrooms and teaching are multidimensional. Pupils (and teachers too) bring multiple concerns, interests and life experiences to the classroom, yet they handle this multiplicity and in the midst of it, for example, learn maths. For the teacher the multidimensional nature of classroom life means they are continually involved in balancing acts, dilemmas and trade-offs.

Classroom events happen simultaneously. Teachers regularly manage more than one event at the same time. They monitor much more than they can report – the 'eyes in the back of the head' phenomenon.

Classroom events are unpredictable in a variety of ways. How will the pupils react? Are they the same as the last lot? What can we do with this new curriculum? Teachers continually handle the ambiguity of knowing that the link between teaching and learning is sometimes uncertain and always partial. There is no single or simple manual, and a vision is crucial for survival: the vision is to make a difference, rather than to be remembered. Increasingly, effective teachers exercise that key skill of modern times – knowing what to do when you don't know what to do.

Where does this analysis lead? Recognising these features has considerable value. Teachers' complex skills are realised and honoured. The nature of classrooms demands high-level skills of interpreting situations and orchestrating learning. Teachers are sometimes slow to describe these aspects, and sometimes feel hesitant to do so lest it divides them from the lay-person. But their professionalism is founded on this complexity.

It also helps us recognise the poverty of those views which portray the classroom as a simple cause-and-effect situation, which offer a simple teacher-centred view, and which propose 'one-size-fits-all' strategies for improvement. These views are common in the voice of policy-makers but are positively dangerous as a basis for improving classrooms. Respectively they lead to teachers feeling de-skilled when simple add-ons don't work, to classrooms not being places where students develop the skills to take responsibility for their learning, and to the creativity of the system being depressed. As noted in Chapter 1, one of the key features of this official voice is its mechanical assumptions. Such discourse is not the voice of teachers, who know only too well that the interaction between teachers and learners and the relations in a classroom are crucial for the quality of classroom life and learning. Yet we live in times when some people seem to believe that all that matters is the measured performance on National Curriculum tests. That's no way to improve: it's more likely to lead to more of the same. As noted analysts of assessment know, the assessment system can be a force which works against change: Patricia Broadfoot[3] puts it like this:

> [To the] change brought about in the schools of the nineteenth century by the . . . advent of public examinations on a mass scale, . . . we owe a century of the class teaching unit, subject-based curricula, didactic pedagogy, extrinsic motivation and norm-referenced assessment.

Teacher–pupil relationships are also highlighted as the crucial issue by Seymour Sarason. In his book *The Predictable Failure of Educational Reform*,[4] he analyses two themes connected to the current focus: the intractability of school systems and the naïvety of reform attempts. His analysis and experience of classrooms leads him to say 'the classroom and the school and school system generally, are not comprehensible unless you flush out the power relationships that inform and control the behavior of everyone in these settings'. He takes the view that these power relations are mirrored at different levels: ' . . . teachers regard students the way their superiors regard them – that is, as incapable of dealing responsibly with issues of power, even on the level of discussion'. It is these dynamics which explain both the intractability and the enduring condition of classrooms:

> In the modal classroom the degree of responsibility given to students is minimal. They are responsible only in the sense that they are expected to complete tasks assigned by teachers and in ways the teachers have indicated. They are not responsible to other students. They are solo learners and performers responsible to one adult.

... The responsibility of the teacher ... is unjustified because it rests on the unexamined and invalid assumption that there are not alternative and productive ways of structuring the social context in which learning can occur, ways that give more responsibility to students.

It is useful to reflect a moment on Sarason's view. I do not conclude that teachers are people who seek to exercise power over groups of folks younger than themselves! Broadly speaking, I find the majority of teachers value and seek more democratic human relations than are found elsewhere. More, I take the view that the current picture of power relations in the classroom is attributable to the complexity of the classroom context together with the dominant view of teaching. These two combine to conspire against teachers' better intentions, and at times they end up using positional power as a coping strategy when they would prefer not to.

Has that ever happened to you? Have you found yourself as a teacher in a classroom, calling on your positional authority when you would have preferred not to? What led to it? What forces encouraged the situation to turn out like this?

The tensions teachers face

The fact that a professional individual can find themselves acting in ways which do not always accord with their professional vision could be explained in a range of ways. A narrow explanation would propose that teachers lack moral fibre – hardly! A very broad view would say that humans often do other than they espouse – probably so. But the stance being developed here is more focused than that: it is to say that the complexity of the classroom and the educational system continually faces teachers with contradictions which are not of their own making but which they must find a way of resolving. When listening at length to how teachers do their work and the dilemmas they face, Stephen Marble[5] and his colleagues portrayed well the situations teachers find themselves in, and the various trade-offs they make. In particular he identified four distinct tensions in how teachers described their work:

- Who is responsible for student performance?
- What does it mean to work with other teachers?
- What is happening in the classroom?
- What is the big picture?

The three specific tensions unfolded along two dimensions each, the polarities of which are described in Table 2.1. Again, this view honours the complexity of teachers' work. The three tensions are all of major importance for the central theme of this book. Power, Teacher relations and Learning.

Teacher agency

I am a little surprised at the extent to which issues of power are important in this introductory analysis. Perhaps my surprise only reflects that I haven't analysed things that way so much in the past, and am only now getting used to it. My current understanding of 'the big picture' in which considerations of teaching sit gives me confidence that power is a crucial issue for the times we're in. At the largest level, influential social theorists like Michel Foucault help us see that society has moved from sovereign power vested in an individual to modern power in which citizens are supposed to police themselves. At the government level, national governments have less power over macroeconomics and turn their attention to domestic domains in order to maintain their claims for potency. In the education domain, successive UK governments have been increasingly prescriptive about practice and thereby reduce the agency of teachers, as well as their morale. In classrooms which succumb to these forces, pupils are seen as having little agency: they are vessels into which a curriculum is delivered. And when teachers are 'made responsible' for the performance of pupils they become more controlling.[6]

Yet a better picture is at hand. This sorry account can be and regularly is reversed, by teachers and pupils who act together in the cause of their own and each others' learning, and recognise that local knowledge is more important than generalised prescriptions handed

Table 2.1 Three tensions in teachers' descriptions of their work

Tension	Dimension		
Responsibility	Authority	⇑⇓	*External* Instructional decisions depend on external policies, conditions or structures
			Internal Instructional decisions are based on personal knowledge of student needs
	Agency	⇑⇓	*Helpless* Student success is independent of teacher action and adjustments to curricula
			Enabled Student success depends on teachers' actions and adjustments to student needs
Professional culture	Professionalism	⇑⇓	*Work* Teaching seen as a job to be done based on application of existing skills
			Profession Teaching seen as a profession that requires continual growth of skills
	Collaboration	⇑⇓	*Solitary* Teaching is a solitary act best done alone in the classroom
			Collegial Teaching is a collegial act best done in collaboration with other teachers and their classrooms
Focus on learning	Sources of knowledge	⇑⇓	*Given* Teachers believe that knowledge is transmitted
			Constructed Teachers believe that knowledge is constructed
	Instructional	⇑⇓	*Didactic* Teachers deliver content complete to students through presentation and lecture
			Facilitative Teacher creates an environment that encourages students to seek knowledge and find personal meaning in that knowledge

to them from afar. We will be hearing some of their stories in later chapters.

One of the key elements in changing classrooms and building learning communities in classrooms is the view of learning which is embodied in the practice. It seems that, as the Stephen Marble study suggested, teachers might have more of or less of a rich view of students' learning, and their part in it. Other studies suggest that this may also be linked to teachers' responses to a changing environment. Susan Stodolsky's studies[7] conclude that teachers who adapt and change are those who 'expressed a very strong commitment to students' personal development and to fostering interpersonal skills'. Such people, who take a wider view of the learner, somehow seem more likely to adapt when, for example, their students change. In what would seem a paradox to the mechanical turn of mind, case studies and surveys conclude: 'Endorsement of goals beyond academic mastery is associated with willingness to adapt instruction'.

At this point let us identify some of the dominant and some of the less dominant views of learning, with an eye to the issue raised above – their richness or breadth.

Views of learning

There are different conceptions of learning, each of which carries different assumptions and implications. These implications for teaching, for curriculum, for assessment and for leading learning, will be discussed throughout this book, which aims to support development towards the third of the three which follow.

Learning = being taught

The most dominant conception of learning relates quickly back to teaching. This is evident when we ask people about their learning experiences: they mostly report occasions of being taught, and focus their description on what the teacher (or equivalent person) has done. In this view, learning is being told. Some people cannot think of learning occasions without a teacher being in the picture. This conception is linked to a view of pedagogy which assumes that learners learn by being told. This in turn is related to the belief that learners acquire new knowledge in predictable and manageable stages. It purports to offer a clear specification of just what it is that is to be learned and, equally questionable, it suggests standards for assessing its achievement. More than any other discourse about learning, this one has spawned 'objectives' and testing in their many guises, and this conception is favoured by policy-makers with short time-scales, curriculum prescriptions of the style seen in the English National Curriculum: 'Pupils will be taught that . . . ', and so on. For short, the term 'instruction' describes this conception. The hazard which is associated with this view is that of leaving the learner out of the picture, or to view them as a passive recipient, and to view teaching as transmission. As Mark Twain put it, 'If teaching was as simple as telling we'd all be a lot smarter than we are'.

Learning = individual sense-making

Another view of learning, which has been the focus of research over the past three decades, brings attention to the processes of the learner in making sense of their experiences, relating them to past experiences and taking learning forward into their future. This view embraces the idea that the learner brings to any new experience their existing understandings and conceptions, so that learning is a process of adaptation based on and constantly modified by their experience of the world. Here, the focus of a teacher moves from the idea that knowledge is transmitted to the idea that it is constructed, and the role of anyone helping (teaching) is examined in terms of how it helps the learner make their own sense. Regarding the learner, this view brings our attention to such things as how an individual learner plans their approach and how they engage in their own sense-making conversation to make learning more effective. For short, this conception is described as 'construction'. A hazard sometimes associated with this view is that it may focus on the individual rather than the social processes the individual is engaged in: in that most complex social environment, the classroom, this point is vital.

Learning = building knowledge through doing things with others

The third stance on learning is described as co-construction. It recognises that all human behaviour has a social dimension, and that knowledge is constructed socially rather than individually. The crucial role of language and conversation in the creation and negotiation of shared meaning is emphasised. The concept of culture is active, since humans are surrounded by the cultural objects in which meaning has been vested by previous generations. And the context in which meaning-making happens comes to be more important, with more attention being paid to the processes by which learning communities are built. This view illuminates such examples as a classroom in which participants are working to create new and shared knowledge on an agreed focus, or a commercial company (especially those in fast-moving industries) which benefits from seeing itself as a knowledge-creating organisation. It helps us see how our current world has become partly characterised as in a 'knowledge explosion', and also that traditional 'bodies of knowledge' are largely made consistent through a community which has ways of agreeing as well as differences. In this view, someone involved in promoting learning will be helping learners engage in 'generative' rather than 'passive' learning activities, and will act on the assumption that learners need to engage in collaborative argumentation and knowledge-testing. The co-construction stance moves us from viewing learning as an acquisition, whatever the commodity to be acquired, to view learning as also becoming part of a community.[8] It would be a hazard of this view to focus solely on social processes to the point of excluding individual ones.

Distinguishing the above three conceptions of learning is valuable for developing a more comprehensive understanding of how learning happens (as opposed to how it is commonly talked about in the official voices). As we progress through the three, more elements are incorporated, especially the learner's role and the social processes: these are crucial and influential elements in classroom and school life.

So how do we see teaching?

There is of course a vast literature which seems to address this question. Much of it tries to paint inspiring answers, some of it offers technical answers, and so on. However, the reality of many classrooms and the patterns of classroom life are often not found in their pages. At work is another set of forces which can have a much stronger everyday impact, and that's why the question is how do we *see* teaching. At any time in history we may see things in different dominant ways, and we are currently in times when the hazard is to see teaching as the teacher's 'planned delivery of the curriculum'. The official voice only focuses on this, but any teacher knows there is a lot more to it. John Sullivan,[9] a teacher of English, puts it like this:

> Due to the inherent uncertainties and anxieties of teachers' professional lives, the tendency is to secure things, to write things down. We want procedures. We want rules. We want our schemes of work written down. Yet all of these produce cultures of control, not cultures of learning. All of these contribute to the idea of learning, of teaching, of **being** in a school as static, rather than dynamic: ventriloquy.

In the particular approach to inspection and accountability which is current, teaching is LOOKED AT in ways which are hazardous for the profession. The hostile witness enters the classroom, focuses on the teacher and focuses on the negative. And sadly, teachers can adopt a similar gaze towards their professional colleagues.

Seeing teaching takes practice. A context-relevant way of looking at teaching recognises that teachers manage classrooms by establishing and running activity systems of various sorts. In the process other key conditions of the classroom are also created: as Walter Doyle[10] said: 'if an activity system is not established and running in a classroom, no amount of discipline will create order'.

It now becomes possible to see some of the differences in teaching as differences in the activity systems which are set up. Some years ago, I answered the deliberately naïve question, 'What does the teacher have in the classroom with which to facilitate the learning of pupils?' with the overlapping headings of Figure 2.1.

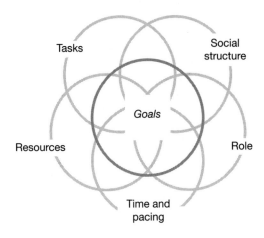

Figure 2.1 The elements of classroom activity systems

This is a general model which can accommodate and describe all the things which are often called 'teaching methods'. More recently[11] I have used it to indicate that the style of activity systems in a classroom might be reflecting the different views of learning which were elaborated earlier. It goes like this:

1   The *instruction* approach to learning puts the focus on the teacher: they design tasks for many pupils, often focusing on what they are to be told and what they are to produce (the processes in between may not be accentuated). Teacher chooses the material and other resources, and plans the timing. When the teacher is 'delivering the curriculum' the pace at which they perform is seen as key.

2   The *construction* approach to learning puts the focus on the learner: tasks emphasise pupils' thinking and processing, and pupils are encouraged to help each other raise questions and show understanding. Here, student experience is seen more as a resource for learning, both experiences outside the classroom and those within. The teacher is more involved in dialogues of enquiry, and the periods of time spent on a topic are often longer.

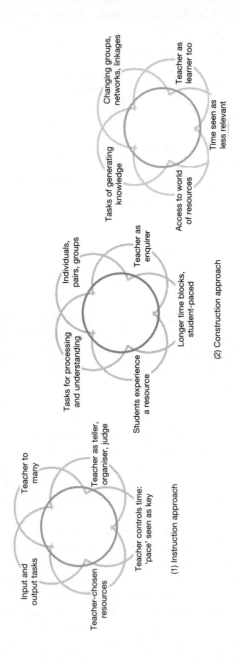

Figure 2.2 Classroom activity systems in three views of learning

(1) Instruction approach

- Teacher to many
- Teacher as teller, organiser, judge
- Teacher controls time: 'pace' seen as key
- Teacher-chosen resources
- Input and output tasks

(2) Construction approach

- Individuals, pairs, groups
- Teacher as enquirer
- Longer time blocks, student-paced
- Students experience a resource
- Tasks for processing and understanding

(3) Co-construction approach

- Changing groups, networks, linkages
- Teacher as learner too
- Time seen as less relevant
- Access to world of resources
- Tasks of generating knowledge

3   The *co-construction* approach to learning puts the focus on the class as a community of learners: tasks are about creating knowledge as well as building criteria for judging that knowledge. A wider variety of linkages are made between members of the class as they contribute to the connected pool, and linkages to others sources of knowledge in the world are rich.

And what's a community?

The term 'community' has been used in more or less helpful ways. Sometimes – and this is one of the more unhelpful ones – it is used to refer to a geographical area. Examples appear in such phrases as 'the school and its community' or 'a community school', which use the term 'community' to denote an unspecified area and perhaps group of people, and at the same time seem to imply that the school will not be referred to as a community. In this book, community will *not* be used to refer to a neighbourhood or other geographical area.

Other uses of the term are more helpful in that they refer to a collective of people, but go little further than that. Here the term can be used in a non-specific fashion which often attracts a sentimental glow (see the next chapter). Examples appear when a school is referred to as a learning community, yet the reference is very vague and the term 'learning community' has become an unjustified synonym for school. In this book, community will not be used in sentimental or non-specific ways.

The most helpful uses of the term refer to

community as a collective, in which each member is an
    Active participant, a sense of
    Belonging has developed,
    Collaboration between members of the community is frequent,
       and
    Diversity of members is embraced.

These hallmarks of community form part of my 'ABCD model'. In this book, classrooms will be referred to as communities of this sort. Also, as we shall see in the next chapter, specific meanings of the term 'learning community' will be developed, as the model is elaborated further.

As a closing thought on this chapter, I return to the modal state of classrooms. One insight from anthropological research on classrooms is that:

> Much of the distinctive nature of the teachers' strategies for handling interaction in the classroom was derived from the nature of the context in which they worked, . . . both the immediate situation of the classroom itself and the organisational setting of the school. . . . In general terms they appeared to have little or no influence on the construction of the timetable . . . , the content of the curriculum, the formation of classes and the allocation of themselves and the pupils to the classes.[12]

So teachers are people who do not choose who they work with, or in what combinations, nor do the pupils they work with choose their teachers or their combinations. In the face of this there are two broad responses. The first is to feel disempowered by this lack of choice: I consider this response is somehow implicated in the way that the dominant classroom does not engage the social collective, staying mainly as a collection of disconnected individuals. The second response embraces the fact that many people are brought together – 'thrown together' even – and utilises this togetherness to contribute to our educational goals. It recognises the core process of learning as the core process of the collective.

Prompts for reflection

Before you turn the page, let's use this chapter break to stop the flow and think about the issues in this chapter.

- Did the three views of learning resonate with your experience? And the three ways of running classrooms?
- Which is the dominant one in your current experience?
- When have you found examples of the non-dominant ones?

How did the teachers in those examples manage to resolve the tensions of teaching in a way which helped them run classrooms differently?

Try this activity:

1   Collect some photographs of classrooms, spanning decades if you can. From what is observable, what has changed over time? What has not?
2   Collect some teachers' memories of classroom life, spanning decades. From their view, what has changed? What has not? What 'pseudo-changes' have they seen come and go?

3   Community – more than a warm glow

In this chapter, I aim to communicate:

1   the way in which the term 'community' is meant in this book;
2   how it contrasts with some other terms;
3   the importance of the concept for schools in current times;
4   an outline of key processes.

The term 'community' offers a view of a classroom or of a school which highlights the forms of relationship in that collective. One of the difficulties with the term, however, is that it never seems to be used unfavourably. Further, it can be used in a way which lacks detail. On these occasions it carries a diffuse warm glow. I find non-specific and romantic uses of the term lack credibility: they paint a picture where goals are non-problematic, relations are always good, and so on – the idyll.

Similarly, if the term 'community' is to highlight working relationships, and, more importantly, learning relationships, there could be difficulties in using the term 'relationships' in a non-specific way. For example, we hear people say they want young people to learn about relationships – do they mean *any* relationship? abusive relationships? and so on? Probably not, but they forget to specify that they really want young people to learn about constructive relationships. The adjective is important. So too with community: what sort of community? A fanatical community or an appreciative community?

As noted in the previous chapter, classrooms are unique social situations. Their crowded and busy nature accentuates issues of relationships, so the way in which we see and build the social relations in that context is of great importance. Teachers realise this in many ways. When I ask teachers to tell me what is most important about life in their classrooms, the answer is regularly that of social relations. Yet many of the current or dominant ways of talking about classrooms do not help us see these aspects. Indeed, many voices on the classroom are silent about the forms of relationships which might best serve that context. By saying nothing they unwittingly promote an undifferentiated view of classroom relations, and collude with unhelpful images – the classroom as a crowd? as a horde? an assortment? an anonymous batch to be processed? All these words say little about the relations between members, or indeed the purposes which may inform those relationships. As a result, the very issue of constructive learning relationships can slip from view.

Community – what metaphor?

Ways of talking about community often call on other images, as in metaphor where our understanding uses one experience to illuminate another. Some of the metaphors which have been used for schools as communities are less than persuasive. For example, talking about community as like family. This metaphor often conveys a rosy view of family, but some of the romanticism that is conveyed about families concerns me, given the evidence that families can be the arenas for destructive experience. Additionally, talking about community as locality: this use is very common in phrases like 'school–community relations', where the word signifies a local neighbourhood. In light of the fact that education has a function of broadening horizons, and going beyond the local to connect to world-wide communities, this metaphor could be peculiarly restrictive.

If there is a single metaphor that comes closest to what I want to convey, it is that of community as orchestra – or band, or even group. This makes the point that people are brought together for a purpose. The relations between members of this collective are highlighted not for their own sake but for the joint action that is to follow. Together they create something that is more than the sum of the parts, and develop real skill in orchestrating both individual and group performance. The musicians are together for a purpose, not because blood relation or quirk of geography binds them. If we see a classroom or a school in these terms, we will see more of the important relations. Of course there are limits to this metaphor, and if we were to accentuate the performance aspect of the orchestra rather than the learning that goes on to create it, or the fact that they are working to someone else's compositions, we would be building an inappropriate image of the learning. John Harvey-Jones, noted chief executive of a number of large companies, took this view:

> the task of managing and leading people is much more akin to being the conductor of an orchestra or a large band or the producer of a film, than being an engineer assembling and running a machine, or an accountant.[1]

He also recognised the importance of situations for the orchestra and leadership:

> A concert is much more than the sum of the parts; the interaction with the audience, the effect of the concert hall and the whole ambience are all parts of the conductor's repertoire which enable him or her to achieve a unique and soaring performance.

Metaphors illuminate by proposing similarities, and we also sometimes clarify by making contrasts. What does the term 'community' contrast with? The answer could be any term for a collective which does not highlight relationship. Contenders include the words we use every day in schools – class, for example. Or, thinking back to the first school in which I taught, where the year groups were divided into smaller units, 'divisions' (on reflection they probably were). On further reflection, the term 'year group' is another of the administrative terms used in a taken-for-granted way: used as such it risks downplaying the very issues of working and learning relationships between members of the collective which they are there to achieve.

Community – an approach to organisations

Thinking about schools customarily uses the language, ideas and assumptions of formal organisation theory – roles, job descriptions, organisation charts, plans and so on – in a taken-for-granted way. This is one impact of the twentieth century, during which we have been taught to think of schools as formal organisations and behaviour within them as organisational behaviour. When analysed, many of the assumptions of this view are mechanical rather than human: they derive from the planning of factories for profit, rather than human association for learning. The mechanical way of thinking is ingrained in our everyday conceptions of organisation and order: we assume a state of orderly relations between clearly defined parts. The presentation of one's school in this rational way may be strategically important: 'Organising schools into departments and grade levels, developing job descriptions, constructing curriculum plans, and putting into place explicit instructional delivery systems of various kinds are all examples of attempts to communicate that school knows what it's doing'.[2]

The machine approach to organisations works well in conditions where machines work well: when the task is straightforward, the environment is stable, and the same product is required repeatedly. Is this conception adequate for schools today?

More than a century ago, Ferdinand Tönnies,[3] a German sociologist and philosopher, drew a distinction between two fundamentally different kinds of institutions:

* *gesellschaft* – an association of people that is based primarily on the members' rational pursuit of their own self-interests;
* *gemeinschaft* – an association of people that is based primarily on shared purposes, personal loyalties and common sentiments.[4]

Two different visions of collectives such as classrooms or schools now emerge.

Tönnies' distinction is sometimes used as though it described a historical trend, associating *gemeinschaft* with rural and pre-industrial societies and *gesellschaft* with modern society. But both sides of the distinction are applicable to modern times. There is no need to associate community with rural, or to imagine the countryside as an idyll (I grew up in one and remember a dark, cold muddy environment!). Community needs to be understood better in the urban environment, especially since the balance of world population has shifted so that the majority now live in cities. In cities there may be different choices, possibilities for access, and so on, leading to different versions of community.

Each worldview is also associated with contrasting conceptions of getting on in the world. The *gesellschaft* worldview sees 'getting ahead' as an individual endeavour; it emphasises mastery of a set of instrumental skills that enables one to make the right transactions in an impersonal and competitive world. The *gemeinschaft* worldview emphasises a personal and interpersonal world in which collaboration is crucial; it sees composing a life as a relational matter, influenced by family and cultural dynamics. People who have specialised in the *gesellschaft* world may denigrate *gemeinschaft*: they may be impatient for 'outcomes' and 'results' and have not experienced effective communities for learning. They have not realised that good relationships are essential for good results.

I have summarised a little more of how this contrast views organisations such as schools in Table 3.1.[5]

Table 3.1 Contrasting views of organisations

Organisation as community	*Organisation as machine*
Represented as groups, networks	Represented as roles, hierarchy, plans
Organisational success is growth and development	Organisational success is 'smooth running'
Focus on affiliation	Focus on performance
'Diffuse' teacher role	Specialist teacher role
Frequent contacts through many settings	Contact is defined by role
Personal success seen as contributing to learning	Personal success seen as individual 'getting ahead'
Discipline addressed through communication	Discipline addressed through procedure
Motivation through commitment, purpose	Motivation through control, contracts
Curriculum tailoring	Curriculum alignment
Solution-finding	Routine, standards
Works well in dynamic, complex context	Works well in stable, routine context

Schools as communities: ancient and modern

The concept of community has been variously applied to schools for some time. It may be useful to review this as we seek an up-to-date conception. Conceptions of schooling have changed and may continue to change. The following historical progression has been suggested:[6]

- *School as community church.* Here, school is about promoting morality and civic good. In these times (end of the nineteenth century) there may have been more of a religious reverence for school: teaching was viewed as a sacred profession (a view which in England and Wales continued into the middle part of the twentieth century – my mother was thrown out of her teaching job in the 1930s for getting married!).
- *School as factory.* This view creates an economic purpose for school, emphasising selection grading and standardisation. At this time the school is managed by principles which view the organisation as a machine, and teachers are viewed as skilled technocrats. Also at this time the notion of failure is invented.
- *School as hospital.* The view of school as addressing the ills of society developed after the world wars and a wider recognition of the injustice of industrial society. School is to ameliorate these difficulties, and at this time a new language develops: 'pupils at risk', 'the needs of children', and so on. For the first time individualisation of the curriculum is considered.
- *School as knowledge-work organisation.* This is a current and future concept. It embraces the idea that we are in a knowledge-work world, and proposes that the function of school is to help students learn what they need to know in such a world. Curriculum is not to be delivered (and received), but becomes a body of knowledge to be processed and formed by students, who are both workers and customers.

In many ways the impact of the early metaphors continues today, and even such brief descriptions may help you notice contemporary features of schooling. The fact that the term community is used so early in the list deserves reflection if we are to bring it up to date. It refers to a time when school was a key institution in any locality, a location for meeting and for advancing individual and community goals. For example, in the south Wales valleys, school was still somewhat revered and it continued to show its historical connection to that other community centre for advancement and struggle, the working men's institute.

Throughout the twentieth century the concept of school as factory has been dominant in many countries. Factory school communities emerged in the USA as reforms in the 1890s, at which time age-grading, subject specialisation and routinised teaching were increased as part of 'efficiency for progress'.[7] They also emerged in Russia in response to industrialisation and urbanisation.[8]

At the end of the twentieth century, the study of school differences has shown that, although the language of school as factory remains, it does not explain the reality. Studies which were premised on the input–output 'sausage-machine' assumptions, have needed to invoke relational and cultural aspects of school such as 'ethos' in order to explain their findings.[9] Research has identified practices and processes in schools which are measurably operating more like a community,[10] and has added practical significance to the vision.

At the beginning of the twenty-first century key challenges face schools and their function which make the idea of a learning and knowledge-creating community more salient. In the contemporary context:

- The knowledge base in society is increasing rapidly, and now said to double every 373 days.[11] Teaching knowledge is an anachronism.
- A wider range of the population process and generate knowledge. Information is not the possession of a few 'experts'.
- Employment prospects relate more to the ability to enhance and transfer learning. The accumulation of qualifications is not enough.
- The landscape of learning is much wider and richer, involving multiple contexts, modes and sources. Learning is no longer the province of special institutions: it is a way of being.

Our up-to-date conception of community must consider the role of communications technology. Although many siren voices warn us of the detrimental impact of new technology on community relationships, other voices see positive potential. For example:

New technologies make it possible to sustain relationships – either directly or indirectly – with an ever-expanding range of other persons. . . . With the intensifying saturation of the culture, however, all our previous assumptions about the self are jeopardised: traditional patterns of relationship turn strange.[12]

Certainly my own experience of easy two-way communication with people around the world and one-way linkage to many others with common interests gives me a changed view of self. And

through the technologies of the century, the number and variety of relationships in which we are engaged, potential frequency of contact, expressed intensity of relationship, and endurance through time are all steadily increasing. As this increase becomes extreme we reach a state of social saturation.

'Virtual communities' are much talked about. It remains an open question how much a collective without person contact can be like a face-to-face version. Turns in communication are separated by time, such communication may be differently strategic as there is more time to plan a contribution, and the sense of joint action may be different. In some cases there is less of oneself invested in a virtual community.

In this chapter so far, I have aimed to position and clarify the term 'community' and suggest that the notion has key relevance to schooling for the future. Now it is possible to put in place some elements and characteristics which help us move from community as a nebulous concept. I turn to describe some of the ingredients which are needed for community to be built.

Hallmarks of community

This section is not about to specify rigid preconditions which must be satisfied in full before development can occur. Rather it proposes both some necessary ingredients for community to flourish, and qualities which grow when community is built. These will contribute to the more detailed frameworks for classrooms and schools in later chapters.

Agency

The belief – on the part of all members – that they can and do make real choices and take action, intentionally and knowingly, is the hallmark of agency.[13] This is both needed and developed by coming together in a collective. However, a further step is possible; a personal sense of agency promotes a pro-social orientation, so the individual fosters a communal life. Collective agency can emerge, people's shared beliefs in their collective power to produce desired results.[14] This is developed when interdependence in a community is recognised and fostered. In a classroom the belief in both personal and collective agency needs to be active on the part of teachers and pupils. This would perhaps seem an easy notion to accept from a distance, but classroom customs often compromise it. If agency is low, community slips from the grasp.

Belonging

A sense of being part of the collective and a psychological sense of membership develop in a community. This has significant effects on engagement in the life and purposes of the collective. The degree to which pupils feel a part of school is associated with their degree of interest in class activity, their persistence in difficult work and their academic results.[15] A key dimension of that sense of belonging and membership is whether students feel respect, acceptance, inclusion and support. A rigid interpretation of belonging could be hazardous, as can occur in overemphasising ideas such as 'building class identity'. Such overstating of belongingness to a particular class (or even the school) might ignore the way in which each pupil is a part of many collectives.

Cohesion

As people act and develop a sense of belonging, they develop an investment of themselves for the purposes which are being achieved in and through this collective. In a community, the growth of commitment is reflected in the process of moving from a number of 'I's' to a 'we'. Again the development of cohesion in a community should not be overstated. It is not a form of compliance, or of 'group-think'. Although there may have been times in history when particular communities set up strong boundaries, these were not communities with a purpose of learning. A sense of cohesion at a sufficient level for joint action is enough, especially because the risk would be of compromising the following condition.

Diversity

In a community setting, differences are not a threat, whereas in the mechanical worldview they probably are. The ability to embrace difference and to view diversity positively is a crucial ingredient. With it, two linked things happen: the risk of stereotyping reduces (and the hazard of division associated with it), and the building of complexity is enhanced. Complexity, the development of which is a guiding principle in education, comes about from two simultaneous developments: a keener sense of difference and differentiated understanding, together with a larger sense of meaning and 'big picture'. The two processes of generating diversity and building cohesion need to go hand-in-hand in order to achieve the balance described as 'unified diversity'.[16] In a school setting with its rushed life and reduced communication, the chance of stereotyping is considerable, especially between teachers and pupils. Images of the other are constructed and acted upon. Yet the reality is more diverse. When pupils are deemed to be unmotivated and disengaged, closer listening to those young people shows they may at the same time have a clear view on their cultural identity and the practices they would honour, as well as seeking to meet wider worlds through the context of school. This offers clues for creating school communities built on difference rather than homogeneity and to become an 'inclusive community of difference'.[17]

Processes in community

Acting together

Activity versus passivity is a dimension of life and learning that has a long history: as recently as 1916, John Dewey argued 'that the school environment be equipped with agencies for doing . . . to an extent rarely attained'.[18] So if a community is about facilitating its members' action, it is also about the fact that to act in community is to act together, to act in concert. Not in unison but with some degree of coordination, sufficient to achieve the additive sense that acting together achieves more than acting alone, and the whole is greater than the sum of the parts. Within this, individual projects take their place as contributing to a whole when the community project for action emerges. Although some elements may emerge which could be (mis)interpreted as elements of the machine organisation, such as division of labour and agreed roles, these are always subservient to the emergent community project. In these conditions members of a collective spend effort in maintaining togetherness and addressing the tensions it sometimes brings:[19] they may do things which to the mechanical observer are 'off-task' but which serve to maintain togetherness and build interdependence in action.

Bridging

Communities connect. This statement obviously applies to the connections and communications which emerge in face-to face interaction, as one person's interests and ideas start to bridge with those of another person. As different individual worlds meet and start to form a collective world, it is important to think of this in a way which maintains the hallmarks of cohesion and diversity. Simple notions such as 'group-think', 'the group mind' or uniform ideas of a group identity do not capture the variation which maintains in community life. But bridging goes further than that and refers to connections made to other parts of life and to other communities. Members of communities know more of the picture of each other in wider parts of life than do members of machine organisations. And they also seem to regularly make connections to similar networks in other places, whether these are other networks of interests or other knowledge communities. The fact that they do not create impermeable walls around them also reflects how processes often described as 'bonding' in discussions of group-building, are inappropriate for a community. The origins of the 'bonding' idea in explaining animal behaviour make plain why it is a reductionist idea to apply to human behaviour.

Collaboration

Cooperation occurs between free agents under some particular conditions: they must feel that their futures are in some way connected.[20]

But such cooperation may remain strategic and take place without a sense of belonging ever developing. Collaboration is a more extended process than cooperation, because it needs people to bring something important together: in communities this is likely to be something of themselves. Bringing something comparable together and working to find common ground are both key ingredients of collaboration. If 'Cooperation is working together to accomplish shared goals'[21] then collaboration is working together on a common task towards a common outcome.[22]

Cooperation between some parties can sometimes be associated with increased competition between them and others, even in some cases of teacher collaboration.[23] Collaboration is less likely to be associated with competition of a between-group sort.

Dialogue

The human capacity for language and meaning is at its highest in dialogue. But again this is one of those words which is often used loosely, sometimes synonymous with discussion. The following distinctions may help:

* *Discussion* is generally held to be a spoken consideration in a group, but its Latin roots carry a meaning of disputation or agitation, as are evident in the medical use of this word, meaning the act or process of breaking up, or dispersing, a tumour, or the like. Also consider other words from this root: percussion and concussion!
* *Debate* is a form of discourse in which two opposing teams defend and attack a given proposition, often in a formalised manner, or make opposing points. Its conflictual nature is reflected in its root, the Old French *débatre*, to beat. See also batter!
* *Dialogue* describes an exchange of ideas or opinions. The roots of this word are the Greek *dialogos* (*dia* = through; *logos* = speech, word, reason). Compare epilogue, prologue etc.

Dialogue as meaningful exchange of ideas and understandings is doubtless rarer in classrooms and schools than we would wish, but for effective human relations it is a central element.

Processes in a community of learners

The hallmarks and processes described above are likely to be found in any collective which attracts the description 'community' in a meaningful way. But note that the purposes of the community have not yet been specified, nor the members. So what extra do we need to understand in order to best describe a community of learners?

First, some points about the term 'community of learners'. As was mentioned in the preceding chapter, the view of learning embodied in a classroom is a crucial, though often unanalysed and unnoticed, dimension. Those who have pioneered classrooms as communities of learners make explicit a view of learning which is active, strategic, reflective and involving metacognition.[24] Without falling into hair-splitting, the weight of ideas are more towards the second model of learning discussed in the preceding chapter (Learning = Individual sense-making) but handled in a collaborative context. This is perhaps indicated in their discussions of metacognition, which are usually in terms of individuals understanding their own learning. Such metacognition is a crucial and potentially transforming element of a classroom, but I suggest that it is less than what emerges in a 'learning community' which is the community learning about its own learning. I have selected two crucial processes for a community of learners.

Enquiry

If a collective is to operate as a community and if the members of that community are engaged and interested in learning, then enquiry is likely to be emphasised as a means of learning and coming to know.[25] An emphasis on first-hand investigation, both through 'hands-on' experimentation and through the use of reference material, is regularly found.[26] The reason for this is not merely that the teachers and researchers involved choose this as their preferred stance on learning: it is also for the effect it has on relationships in the collective. Enquiry captures key human processes such as interest and questioning, and it does so in a way which supports engagement between people. Enquiry does not invoke right answers or authority-based solutions: instead it invites communication and accepts diversity. Its goal is enhanced understanding.

Established communities of learners have enquiry at their core. Take any of the 'learned societies': they associate in order to exchange and deliberate the results of their enquiries, on occasion coming to agreements about their most effective ways of testing knowledge. They also often associate with others in order to press collaborative enquiry. I think it is no coincidence that a view of learning which highlights the process of making connections between ideas and between areas of knowledge also operates in contexts where connections between people are rich. Take a smaller example of the scientists in a laboratory[27] or a team of photocopier mechanics:[28] their communication and collaborative construction of new knowledge is based around the problems they have posed and the results of their active enquiry.

Knowledge-generation

Learning is a key human process, and at the same time it seems centrally human to seek a product. Here, the product of learning is knowledge: being human is to appropriate knowledge and to produce knowledge.[29] What is meant by 'knowledge' is crucially changing here: it is not the school view – subject matter, taught by teachers and found in books, a commodity, to be amassed and banked[30] – it is a contextually relevant new meaning, often in the form of new understandings for the people involved in learning, but also often placed in some public domain by a performance of understanding which asks students to convey what they know as a way of demonstrating their understanding.[31] So for the process of generation, knowledge is not in heads but in what people create when they get their heads together, not in books or other sources but in what people create when they go to those sources. And the product, although it is in some incomplete sense a representation of the new knowing,[32] is not treated as though it could lead to knowledge being simply transmitted to others through this means; others' interpretation and sense-making is always in the picture as they in turn appropriate from it.

In the knowledge age, the challenge is to 'make knowledge building the principal activity in schooling', where this is understood as encompassing 'both the grasping of what others have already understood and the sustained, collective effort to extend the boundaries of what is known'.[33] One of the helpful concepts in this stance is that knowledge is an improvable object: it is always possible to review our knowledge of anything and agree how our knowledge may be improved.

Processes in a learning community

The adjective which people place before the word 'community' is instructive. Some examples give clear evidence that the writer has not developed the core understandings in this chapter so far, as when the UK Prime Minister writes:

> Strong communities depend on shared values and a recognition of the rights and duties of citizenship – not just the duty to pay taxes and obey the law, but the obligation to bring up children as competent, responsible citizens, and to support those – such as teachers – who are employed by the state in the task. In the past we have tended to take such duties for granted. But where they are neglected, we should not hesitate to encourage and even enforce them, as we are seeking to do with initiatives such as our 'home-school contracts' between schools and parents.[34]

This speaks to me of a *gesellschaft* view of the world, rather than a *gemeinschaft* view on which the word community is based.

By contrast, some of those who use the term 'caring community' do so in a way which is much more specific than the 'warm glow' they seek to develop for children

> their kindness and considerateness, concern for others, interpersonal awareness and understanding, and ability and inclination to balance consideration of their own needs with consideration for the needs of others, as well as their intrinsic motivation and attainment of higher-level academic skills[35]

and have identified the practices and outcomes of such (see the following chapters).

At this point I wish to consider a learning community, but the adjective here is not to be used in the weak sense, in the way that learning community is used merely as a synonym for school. I use the adjective in a strong sense so that learning community means a collective that is collectively learning, including about its own processes of learning. In this sense I feel it is an important addition to much of the already inspiring literature and practice on communities of learners, which I now view by contrast as collectives of learners which may be learning collaboratively, but mainly about the knowledge questions in hand, and not necessarily about their own learning. In this sense I identify the following two processes which are present in learning communities.

Reflection

For individuals and collectives to be able to learn from experience, reflection is essential. It is the only route through which our experience can be made an object of knowledge. Reflection is often spoken about as an individual phenomenon: in this sense numerous studies demonstrate how it may be promoted[36] and its significant contribution to individual performance: the GCSE scores of pupils who reflect least are 30 per cent of the scores of those who reflect most.[37] But a community demonstrates its organic rather than mechanical nature by learning from the experience of its own workings. At such moments many of the key elements such as agency, dialogue and enquiry are present to the full.

In a learning community there will be collective reflection, not as a substitute for individual reflection but growing from and enhancing it. This may comprise collective reflection about the enquiries in hand, but may crucially be extended to collective reflection about the community processes for enquiring and learning. The practices this requires in a classroom are rarely reported in the literature on classrooms.

Meta-learning

The term 'metacognition' has a relatively short history,[38] but a very important role in individual learning. Strictly, metacognition is thinking about thinking: here I use the term 'meta-learning' to denote learning about learning. This is clearly a much wider set of considerations than just thinking, and encompasses learning about goals, strategies, feelings, effects and contexts of learning.[39] For these times of overemphasising pupil performance, I have reviewed elsewhere[40] the contribution that enhanced meta-learning makes to individual performance, the contribution is notable, including for learners deemed 'learning disabled'[41] or 'having learning difficulties'.[42] And the classroom practices are identifiable. At the individual level, meta-learning is shown to be crucial for that much-claimed but often absent element: transfer. Not only for knowledge generated in a classroom to be applied in similar situations outside the classroom, but also for the understandings and capacities in learning which may have developed, meta-learning is essential.

Again, in a learning community there will be collective meta-learning. This requires as a necessary element the collective reflection referred to above, but extends it into new meaning, understanding and knowledge of learning communities.

A summary of key elements

The key elements reviewed in this chapter may be summarised as in Figure 3.1

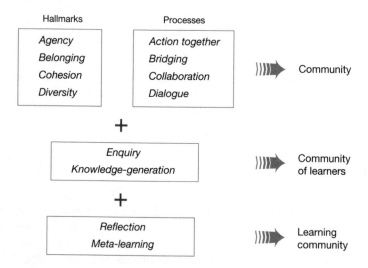

Figure 3.1 Key elements in learning community

Prompts for reflection

- Do you find the word 'community' used in more and less useful ways? When you want to convey something through the use of that term, what is it that's special for you?
- Recall some of the occasions when a classroom you know has shown some of the qualities of a community. How did this happen? What did you learn from these occasions?
- Have you ever experienced a learning community? What happened that leads you to describe it that way?
- If you have not experienced what you think a learning community is, can you develop those thoughts into more detail as to what it would be like?

Having outlined and hopefully clarified the vision of community which might be transportable into a classroom, you may be ready to examine the classroom practices which contribute to such a development. These are to be found in Chapters 5 to 9. But before that it may be useful to review what is known about the impact of operating classrooms in the ways outlined so far. That is the focus of Chapter 4. In part, the evidence reviewed there is another answer to the question of this book series: 'What's in it for schools?', but we should take care with that question lest the institution appears to become the primary entity for attention. Schools exist for pupils and the society they will compose, and we must beware falling into the situation described by one pupil in a research project who said, referring to his teachers, 'They used to care about us – now they care about them'. So the review may also answer 'What's in it for pupils?'.

4 Classrooms as learning communities

A review of research

The point of this chapter is to review published research on classrooms as learning communities, and thence to get a better idea of the effects of operating classrooms in this way. The voices from research are one part of the answer to 'What's in it for schools?'.

The style of writing for this chapter differs somewhat from the others: it is more about findings than about visions and practices. This is deliberate, as I want no one reading this review to be left in any doubt about the messages from research.

Operating classrooms as learning communities may not be the dominant style, and may be correspondingly under-researched, but from a reading of about 100 texts there is good evidence that it brings significant benefits.

The focus of this review is stimulated by answers to the larger question 'What helps learning in classrooms?'. Various meta-analyses have brought together multiple studies of classroom learning. One, covering 11,000 statistically significant findings,[1] showed that the way in which the classroom is managed is more influential than any other variable. This points to the teachers' role in composing a classroom which attends to both social relations and learning, and the social nature of classroom management. More recently an analysis which combined studies on over a million learners[2] arrived at two conclusions which confirm the focus here: 'Metacognition is the engine of learning', so that thinking and reflection are key processes for the classroom, and 'the self-system appears to be the control center for human behavior' so that how the classroom engages learners' beliefs and learners' control is crucial. Class-rooms as learning communities aim to embrace both these conclusions.

Classrooms vary in the ways they operate and their variation may be understood in terms of the approach to learning which is in operation.[3] The dominant approach is 'Learning = being taught', with its associated language of transmission and delivery. In a smaller number of classrooms the view 'Learning = individual sense-making' operates. This accords with the findings of twentieth-century research on human understanding. In the fields of mathematics and science education, much research adopts this constructivist view of learning (despite the fact that the folk view of these subjects holds strongly that they are about facts and knowledge rather than sense-making).[4, 5] The evidence that teachers who adopt beliefs and practices along the constructivist lines get better results than those who adopt beliefs and practices along the lines of 'Learning = being taught' now covers a range of countries and age groups: for example, 6-year-olds in the USA,[6] 9-year-olds in Germany,[7] 10-year-olds in Japan[8] and secondary school students.[9]

The research to be considered here goes beyond the idea of learning is individual sense-making, towards the view that learning is constructing knowledge with others. 'In a learning community the goal is to advance the collective knowledge and, in that way, support the growth of individual knowledge'.[10] It positions learning as a process of negotiation among the individuals in a learning community, and sees individual learning as rooted in the culture within which the individual learns.[11] In learning communities, social relations and knowledge-creation meet. Knowledge (both individual and shared) is seen to be the product of social processes.

There are fewer studies than one might reasonably expect of classrooms which develop in this style. Much classroom research reflects the dominant conception of 'Learning = being taught', and investigates matters such as teachers' questioning, teachers' managing the classroom, teachers' dealing with student misbehaviour, teachers' grouping of pupils, etc. Thus is a teacher-centred view of classroom life maintained, together with an anonymous view of learners in which research questions such as 'Is it best to seat them in rows or groups?' are posed. Nevertheless there is a significant body of research which shows that paying attention to social relations and learning processes brings considerable dividends – in short, better learning, better performance and better behaviour.

The school as a context for classrooms

Classrooms rarely operate as separate islands, and one of the major influences on them is the culture of the school. Research findings on schools as communities provide a backdrop for the focus on classrooms.

Some schools operate more as communities than do others. This difference makes a difference to a range of behaviours and capacities as learners. Secondary schools that score high on an index of communal organisation

> attend to the needs of students for affiliation and . . . provide a rich spectrum of adult roles [that] can have positive effects on the ways both students and teachers view their work. Adults engage students personally and challenge them to engage in the life of the school.

Such schools show higher teacher efficacy, morale and enjoyment, and students in such schools are more interested in academics, absent less often, and there are fewer behaviour difficulties.[12] A study of 11,794 16-year-olds in 830 secondary schools revealed that students' gains in achievement and engagement were significantly higher in schools with practices derived from thinking of the school as a community, rather than the common form of thinking of the school as a bureaucracy.[13] Similar findings apply to primary schools: those where students agree with statements such as 'My school is like a family' and 'Students really care about each other' show

> a host of positive outcomes. These include higher educational expectations and academic performance, stronger motivation to learn, greater liking for school, less absenteeism, greater social competence, fewer conduct problems, reduced drug use and delinquency, and greater commitment to democratic values.[14]

Pupils' sense of the school as a community has been measured with validity, and relates to individual matters such as motivation. A study of 301 students in the early secondary years concluded 'a student's subjective sense of belonging appears to have a significant impact on several measures of motivation and on engaged and persistent effort in difficult academic work'.[15] School sense of membership is strongly associated with pupils' valuing of schoolwork, their general school motivation, expectancy of success and self-reported effort. These motivation-related measures are more associated with the sense of belonging to school than they were with their friends' valuing of school, thereby challenging the folk theory of 'peer pressure' as most influential in motivation.[16]

Students with a higher sense of school membership report higher grades, and a more internal locus of control, the sense that success was more in their hands than in the hands of others.[17] This last element can be seen as evidence against interpreting sense of school membership as a simple idea of compliance to organisational rules – the characteristics of the school matter. Similarly, sense of belonging to school is not limiting students to their school: it is associated with looking ahead and expectations for the future.[18] Positive feelings about school relate to positive teacher–student relationships, but more so when there is a feeling of school belonging. Additionally, sense of school belonging is positively related to academic grades, and even more so when students feel that school focuses on learning and on improving competence rather than on performance and proving competence.[19] Higher levels of affiliation to school reflect students' current participation in school, not their history of prior achievement.[20]

Students' sense of school membership influences their patterns of behaviour outside school as well as inside. Schools with higher average sense-of-community scores had significantly lower average student drug use and delinquency, suggesting that schools that are experienced as communities may enhance students' resiliency.[21] School supportiveness, sense of community, and opportunities for students to interact and to exert influence are key factors.[22] A survey of 36,254 13- to 18-year-old students showed that school connectedness (more so than family connectedness) was the most salient protective factor against behaviours such as drug use, school absenteeism, pregnancy risk and delinquency risk.[23] Analysis of 12,118 follow-up interviews concluded '[W]e find consistent evidence that perceived caring and connectedness to others is important in understanding the health of young people today'.[24]

School differences are also set in a larger picture across countries, indicating that schools operate more as communities in some countries than in others. In a recent survey of representative samples in 42 countries, 224,058 15-year-olds in 8,364 schools were asked to respond to 'My school is a place where I feel like I belong'. Seventy-nine per cent affirmed this statement, but country differences ranged from France (44 per cent), Spain (52 per cent) and Belgium (53 per cent), to Australia (85 per cent), Finland (86 per cent) and Hungary (89 per cent).[25, 26] Within countries, school differences were significant: 'In nearly every country, there is a wide range among schools in the prevalence of students considered to have a low sense of belonging and low participation'. This variation is not explained by 'family background' of students but suggests aspects of school policy and practice create student disaffection. *For schools*, sense of belonging is moderately correlated with student performance in reading, mathematics and science. 'So schools which give priority to working on student engagement do not do so at the expense of developing such skills as literacy – schools that have strong student engagement tend to have strong literacy performance'. *For any individual*, sense of belonging may not be strongly related to performance: disengaging from school does not result in poor academic performance in all cases. Disengagement from school is not simply about academic success: school practices matter.

Sense of school community can be enhanced for both students and teachers, and the route is through the classroom rather than through extra-curricular programmes or activities. 'These findings suggest that students will not sign up for those activities unless they already experience themselves as being part of a supportive community'.[27] Such programmes are known to make a difference: 'Effects were strongest for students in the subset of schools that had made the greatest degree of progress in program implementation'.[28]

The benefits of community building in schools are not achieved through building any sort of community. Much depends on the values which develop, and the best is achieved through a caring, pro-social, learning-oriented approach to the relations between all parties. And this strategy is relevant for those schools which are sometimes portrayed as most difficult: 'the potential benefits of enhancing school community may be greatest in schools with large numbers of economically disadvantaged students'.[29] The benefits are often lasting, from primary schools persisting through secondary school[30] on achievement test scores, academic engagement, social skills and misbehaviour.

The classroom

Focusing now on the classroom, this review will not concentrate so much on the detail of teachers' classroom practices (see Chapters 5 to 9) as on the effects.

The review begins with research into (A) classrooms as communities, then (B) classrooms as communities of learners, then (C) classrooms as learning communities. These sections are in some sense cumulative, since the development of classroom communities is concerned with both social and academic outcomes, and sees them as connected. Indeed it has been argued that the agenda for education reform should reflect all three of the forthcoming sections and should cover 'social, ethical, and civic dispositions; attitudes toward school and learning motivation; and metacognitive skills'.[31]

(A) Classrooms as communities

(1) In classrooms where a sense of community is built, students are crew, not passengers

In any collective which operates as a community, all participants are active, so in a classroom community students are treated as active agents in collaboration to promote learning. The exercise of human *agency* is about intentional action, exercising choice, making a difference and monitoring effects.[32] The collaboration on which classrooms as communities depend requires that students are active agents in choosing and learning:

> We propose that the engine of collaboration is agency and its expression in the effort to represent and share in other people's thoughts. . . . One way this agency is expressed is by the decision to collaborate and the effort to reach an understanding when social rules are insufficient for successful collaboration. Another way agency is expressed is by the motivation to produce and contribute. Finally, productive agency appears in the very way we learn – we construct knowledge.[33]

Human learning is about both appropriating and producing knowledge, yet the dominant model of classrooms does not start with practices which enhance student agency. To create higher levels of agency for children is the challenge of creating classrooms that are knowledge-building environments. To find ways in which student choice and student ideas are developed has been identified as a key issue in the design of ICT support.[34]

Emphasis on community action is sometimes portrayed as in tension with emphasising achievements of individuals, but the evidence does not support such a view. An eminent researcher in this field concludes:

> The findings taken as a whole show that the higher the perceived collective efficacy, the higher the groups' motivational investment in their undertakings, the stronger their staying power in the face of impediments and setbacks, and the greater their performance accomplishments.[35]

(2) *In classrooms where a sense of community is built, pupils act as part of a larger whole*

Participation in school is an outgrowth of student sense of belongingness. Generally this is weakly influenced by typical aspects of the effects of school leadership and organisation.[36] It is influenced by both peers and teachers, more so than by parents in a study of teachers, parents and 1,500 pupils aged 9 to 16.[37]

Classroom involvement and participation are linked to a sense of community; as students' sense of community increases, participation increases. By encouraging supportive relationships among students through cooperative learning activities, student satisfaction with the group increases and behavioural referrals drop by as much as 71 per cent.[38] Students indicated a greater ability to build relationships, and worry less about 'being put down'. In informal activities, good relations became more widespread and factions became less in evidence.

Greater motivation also comes with increased relatedness in communities. Both intrinsic academic motivation and autonomy were related to students' sense of community in a longitudinal study of 4,515 students of ages 9 to 12 in multiple schools and districts.[39] This was explained in terms of three core interrelated motivations: perceived competence, sense of control and perceptions of autonomy.[40] 'The higher the perceived quality of relatedness, the greater one's feelings of autonomy and competence'.[41] So relatedness and autonomy are not opposites, as they are sometimes depicted. The three motivational variables in turn predicted children's performance as measured by grades, achievement and teacher ratings of competence. Students involved in a programme to develop community scored significantly higher than comparison students in sense of efficacy during middle school. 'Program students also had significantly higher grade-point-averages and achievement test scores than comparison students'.[42]

Engagement and relatedness also influence risk behaviour. As students feel more supported they become more engaged and this in turn reduces risk behaviour and likelihood of dropping out.[43] In this longitudinal study of 443 urban African-American adolescents, engaged students reported more positive perceptions of competence, autonomy and relatedness in the school setting than did students who were less engaged.

(3) In classrooms where a sense of community is built, relations are about 'we' rather than 'you and me'

Classrooms which operate as communities encourage children to take an active role in classroom governance. The authority structure of the classroom is an important determinant of students' experience of community and of some of its observed effects.[44] Comparison of two contrasting programmes has shown that the style of governance makes a difference:

> Although teachers in both of the programmes stressed the importance of positive student behaviour, this appears to have been defined more as *diligence, compliance and respect for authority* in the [external standards] school, and more as *interpersonal helpfulness, concern and understanding* in the [classroom community] schools.[45]

Ten-year-olds' interpersonal behaviour was more helpful and supportive in the latter.

Through practices such as the class meeting to discuss issues of concern, pupils work collaboratively with the teacher to develop solutions to discipline problems. Teachers avoid extrinsic incentives (rewards as well as punishments) so that children will develop their own reasons for positive actions other than 'what's in it for me?'

In general the greater the sense of community among the students in such a class, the more favourable their outcomes on measures of prosocial values, helping, conflict resolution skill, responses to transgressions, motivation to help others learn, and intrinsic motivation.[46]

Teachers' encouragement of cooperative activities appears to be particularly important in teacher practices associated with students' sense of the classroom as a community.[47]

Sense of classroom community is positively related to higher-level moral reasoning based on internalised values and norms, and negatively related to lower-level reasoning based on conformity to authority, social approval or disapproval, or reward and punishment.[48] Students in schools with a strong sense of community are more likely to act ethically and altruistically,[49] and to develop social and emotional competencies.

(4) In classrooms where a sense of community is built, diverse contributions are embraced

When classrooms operate as communities, a wider range of roles becomes available, both for the classroom and for each participant: ' . . . students began to view themselves in different roles and speak about themselves in different ways'.[50]

Patterns of contribution become more balanced than those in teacher-centred classrooms, with individuals whose contribution rates are markedly different in large group settings displaying very similar contribution rates in small groups: '[small groups] provided a more equitable opportunity for its members to participate in high-level discourse about science than did whole-class lessons'.[51]

A wider range of pupils becomes valued. As one teacher put it in an ICT-supported community classroom: 'Instead of being outcasts, the nerdy kids are being treated with reverence. . . . [It] afforded a lot of kids that don't normally have success in school, some success'. And pupils learn a wider range of roles: 'I think there are some kids that facilitate learning, and who want to help. I think it [knowledge-building community] brings this out in some kids that aren't normally helpful or facilitating'.[52]

On dimensions which are typically associated with difference in treatment and valuing in the dominant classroom, classroom communities de-emphasise difference and promote inclusion. The practices and experiences which school students report as promoting membership and belonging for them are the same practices as they see appropriate for their classmates with severe disabilities.[53]

When a range of contributions is valued in the service of a larger whole, possession of ideas and right answers is less important. 'The students put competition and claims of authorship into perspective. Against these, they emphasized that they should work as a community and that it is the idea that matters, not who came up with it in the first place'.[54]

Sense of a classroom as a community can be enhanced over time. For one programme, students scored significantly higher on the measure of sense of community than did comparison students for each of three years.[55]

(B) Classrooms as communities of learners

The social arrangements which create a sense of community in a class-room can operate well but not necessarily implicate the conception of learning which inhabits that classroom. Caring and pro-social classroom communities can continue a teacher-centred view when it comes to learning. The next section reviews studies which have examined the application of community practices to the fact that the members are learners.

(1) In classrooms which operate as a community of learners, engaged enquiry emerges

Agency and belonging in a community of learners are enhanced by the key practice of eliciting learners' questions. Various studies show that when this happens, the intellectual demandingness is high, both in the type of questions and the processes which follow. When students are asked to generate questions at the start of a new topic, they are likely to ask questions derived from their need to understand and focus on things that they are genuinely interested in. Such questions are of a higher order than text-based questions produced after reading.[56] And primary school students are able to follow their questions in depth.[57]

When students direct collaborative knowledge-building discussions on science topics, they have been judged as conforming to canons of scientific enquiry, validated by independent judgements from philosophers of science, confirming that students collectively exhibit a high level of what may properly be called scientific thinking.[58] Similarly in a maths classroom: 'students expressed their real interest and were motivated to work on problems. They engaged in mathematical discussions rather than applying algorithms and textbook rules.'[59]

When such practices are used in a classroom fostering a community of learners, students became passionately engaged, used evidence in scholarly ways, developed several arguments and generated core questions. 'Students' arguments for their claims became increasingly sophisticated over time',[60] leading to the description 'Productive disciplinary engagement'.

(2) In classrooms which operate as a community of learners, students help each other learn

When interaction between members of a class is focused on the topic and process of learning, their relations become more respectful and helpful. One of the leading researchers in this field concluded:

> When an atmosphere of respect and responsibility is operating in the classroom, it is manifested in several ways. One excellent example is turn-taking. Compared with many excerpts of classroom dialogue, we see relatively little overlapping discourse. Students listen to one another.[61]

Further, 'we showed that children, collaborating as members of a community of inquiry, are motivated to help each other and to learn from each other'.[62]

In contrast to the impersonal relations of many classrooms, in which concerns about peer judgement and fear of criticism arise, getting to know other class members leads to a different assessment of the risk of contributing. Trust builds and members become more likely to 'ask questions, express a minority opinion, play the devil's advocate, or publicly wrestle with ideas'.[63]

ICT can make an important contribution to building a community of learners. In one example of the few ICT tools which embody a learning community stance, 'a more even distribution of contributions and greater attention to and productive use of the ideas of collaborators' was demonstrated.[64] Students engaged in more reflective activity when they had both face-to-face activity as well as the collaborative technology to construct and pursue collaborative learning goals.[65]

(3) In classrooms which operate as a community of learners, students show productive engagement and orientation to learn

The correlation between students' sense of community and both intrinsic academic motivation and autonomy is a feature of classrooms as communities (see previous section). In a community of learners students use collaborative enquiry to address authentic questions they have generated, and their agency creates a range of effects: group productivity increases as students gain ownership, cognitive engagement increases as public dialogue centres on discussions of their own experiences, and students take responsibility for learning and teaching as they work in teams. When tasks are student-initiated collaborative interactions in groups increase; by contrast, when students complete teacher-designed activities student dialogue centres more on the procedural aspects of the activity.[66] Under these conditions, when multiple perspectives are reconciled through the medium of dialogue, collaboration creates more abstractions than does individual work.[67]

Sense of community in a classroom also supports a learning orientation on the part of pupils, which is crucial for them to be active engaged learners and for high achievement. At the crucial time of transition between schools it has been shown that the common change in learners' orientation is towards a concern for proving competence rather than improving competence. A longitudinal survey of 660 students indicated that exceptions to this pattern occurred when learners perceived a learning orientation in classrooms, and these occasions are associated with a higher sense of school belonging.[68]

(4) In classrooms which operate as a community of learners, students show better knowledge, understanding, application and transfer

Programmes which aim to foster communities of learners have encouraged pupils to: (i) engage in self-reflective learning and (ii) act as researchers who are responsible to some extent for defining their own knowledge and expertise. The aim is to enhance children's emergent strategies and metacognition, and help them advance each others' understanding in small groups, through processes such as 'reciprocal teaching'.[69]

Results from such classrooms show that improving both literacy skills and subject knowledge improve, specifically:

- 'Domain-specific content is retained better by students'.
- 'Students were able to use information more flexibly in discussing thought experiments' (hypothetical situations) and counter-examples.
- Students were better at applying knowledge: 'Over time the research students introduce more novel variations of taught principles along with more truly novel ideas'.
- Students show better transfer of learning to other domains, through: '(1) improvement in students' reading comprehension scores on materials outside the domain of study and (2) gradual acquisition of increasingly complex forms of argumentation and explanation strategies'.
- Students more than doubled their comprehension on a measure where they answered questions after reading a provided passage unrelated to the curriculum of the class. They 'showed especially strong gains in their ability to summarise a passage and in their ability to solve problems analogous to the one in the provided passage'.
- Students' argumentation skills improved: 'Explanations were more often supported by warrants and backings. The nature of what constitutes evidence was discussed, including a consideration of negative evidence. A variety of plausible reasoning strategies began to emerge'.[70]

This approach goes well beyond attempts to train pupils in learning strategies, when typically there is little evidence of them using strategies when left to their own devices. As the investigator put it:

> Gradually it became apparent that the children's failure to make use of their strategic repertoire was a problem of understanding: they had little insight into their own ability to learn intentionally; they lacked reflection. Children do not use a whole variety of learning strategies because they do not know much about the art of learning.[71]

Thus a key element in communities of learners is that

> students should be active participants in the program, aware of their learning processes and progress. They should come to understand why they are engaging in the activities that form the basis of the program. . . . they should be able to serve as collaborators in the orchestration of their own learning.[72]

The extent to which the gains from these interventions are shown up in public forms of assessment depends on what form is used:

> Two of the most successful schools in our research participated in a state-mandated, high-stakes performance assessment. In contrast to the standardized tests used in the other districts, the assessment was consonant with [the classroom community program's] educational approach, both in its emphasis on higher-order thinking in response to open-ended questions and in its inclusion of collaborative group investigations and problem-solving in science, mathematics, and social studies. . . . Of the six districts studied, only in this district did educators see their community-building effort as a means to promote achievement on mandated assessments.[73]

(C) Classrooms as learning communities

A classroom run as a learning community operates on the understanding that the growth of knowledge involves individual and social processes.

It aims to enhance individual learning that is both a contribution to their own learning and the group's learning, and does this through supporting individual contributions to a communal effort. Here the stance is that the agent of enquiry is not an individual, but a knowledge-building community.[74]

(1) In classrooms which operate as a learning community, disciplined discourse develops

Accounts of classrooms as knowledge-building communities include those with specially designed ICT support. From the earliest examples, 'There have been impressive results in textual and graphical literacy, theory improvement, students' implicit theories of learning, standardized achievement tests, and comprehension of difficult texts. Results appear stronger the longer students use this collaborative environment'.[75] Disciplined discourse emerges: records of a community discussion over a period of three months, comprising 179 entries,[76] show that although it may begin as personally-oriented, it evolves into a scientific enquiry. Students pursue various knowledge sources, and undertake empirical studies so as to test their questions.

(2) In classrooms which operate as a learning community, responsibility for and control of knowledge becomes shared

In this sort of classroom, members not only take responsibility for themselves and others, but also take responsibility for knowing what needs to be known and for ensuring that others know what needs to be known.[77]

The cognitive and the social are both developed in such an environment. Fourteen-year-olds whose class ran as a constructivist learning environment using communal knowledge-building software over a one-year period showed 'a higher level of self-regard, improved ability to regulate their behavior and an increased ability to make credible judgments about someone else's assertions than did the control group'.[78]

(3) In classrooms which operate as a learning community, conceptions of learning are richer and co-constructive

Classrooms which operate as knowledge-building communities are characterised by the interplay of private and public reflection, and in such contexts students change their approach to learning from a shallow passive one to a deeper active one. A total of 110 junior school students in five comparable classes were assessed in terms of their beliefs about learning, and their reading comprehension, six months apart. They became more likely to report that learning is a matter of understanding and not simply getting all of the facts, that it is important to fit new information with what is already known and that learning is a matter of understanding increasingly complex information and not simply a matter of answering all of the questions. These students showed a significant improvement in problem-solving and recall of complex information, and were significantly more likely to use information provided in a text to solve problems.[79]

The shared view of knowledge which develops in a learning community is voiced by 11-year-olds reflecting on their learning:

> Even if you learn something perfectly, or are a pioneer in your area, all your work is useless if nobody else can understand you. You might as well have done no work at all. The point of learning is to share it with others. Lone learning is not enough.[80]

> Good science making is all about working with ideas, testing them out in different conditions, retesting, talking with people who are working on similar ideas, and bringing ideas to the whole group.[81]

(4) In classrooms which operate as a learning community, we understand our learning together

The combination of talking and writing is important in the service of learning: by discussing their understandings students construct more advanced knowledge, and incorporate the outcomes of discussions in their written understandings. Eleven-year-olds have been very positive about talking- and writing-to-learn and also on the combination, which shows an appreciable level of metacognitive awareness.[82] Collective metacognition has been noted emerging in group discussions among 14-year-olds. This includes planning and regulating (including standards for task performance), monitoring (including comments on the status of their understanding), and evaluating (including evaluating others' ideas – positively more often than negatively).[83] In these ways, one hallmark of a learning community is built – it is a community which learns about its own learning.

Again, interventions which focus on running classrooms as learning communities have proved viable, with important results, not the least of which is changing the culture of the classroom. A cumulative effect over three years has been shown in some studies, with the quality of student explanations monotonically increasing over that time, and moving from descriptive in year 1 to explanatory in year 3.[84]

The processes of a learning community can be built without expensive technological support.[85] Indeed, relying on pre-existing technology from outside is not likely to change the dominant culture of classrooms. Technology needs to co-evolve with social practices and structures of participation in communities[86, 87] for effective learning environments to be built.[88]

Prompts for reflection

- Which aspects of the research in this chapter surprise you the most? And which the least?
- Does your reading of this review help you notice anything about your current beliefs regarding young people and regarding classrooms?
- Are there aspects which have been briefly mentioned here which you would like to explore in classrooms you're in?

Concluding this review

This review shows adequate evidence to support the idea that the development of learning communities should be a key feature of twenty-first-century schools. The connectedness of outcomes – social, moral, behavioural, intellectual and performance – is a particularly important feature here, and one which may address the challenge which has been set by key players in this field:

> To draw politicians and business people away from their fixation on achievement test gains one must offer them the vision of a superior kind of *outcome*. The failure to do that is, I believe, the most profound failure of educational thought in our epoch.[89]

At the same time, the fact that the research reviewed here is investigating understandings which are against the current of dominant discourses could create difficulty for both researchers and practitioners alike. Researchers may have to put additional effort into their proposals in this domain. Teachers may find themselves developing practice which is contrary to the conventions of 5,000 years. In a classroom where the aim is to promote public dialogue and deep understanding rather than pre-fixed procedures, close analysis of the discourse confirms that the teacher will find herself amidst various voices which may be in tension or even conflict.[90] But it would be hazardous to overstate or oversimplify these forces. Voices on educational reform show considerable variation, and are not the one simple or single stance which is sometimes stated.

It is noticeable that the research reports span North America, continental Europe and the Far East but none comes from the United Kingdom. The UK has excellent pioneers in aspects of classrooms as learning communities, such as dialogue, thinking and ICT,[91] but there is not a comprehensive framework applicable to all classrooms nor studies of its impact. In addition, I have been unable to find a UK example where school classrooms are using the technology referred to above for building learning communities.

Interlude

Practices in classrooms

My interest in creating this book is to communicate practices in classrooms that support the vision of learning communities. I also want to actively acknowledge that classrooms are necessarily complex and necessarily varied, so there will be no single answer. And I accept that local knowledge of learners must be a guiding light in building classrooms (and leave to those who think they know what is best for everyone the task of specifying what works for all).

So here, in the next five chapters, I need to avoid the pitfall of writing prescriptions which could easily turn out to be like the mechanical fixes promulgated centrally by the official voice. How might I do that? I intend to use two main devices: naïve questions and stories. Both of these stand in contrast to the definitive statements and lists so beloved by mechanical views of classrooms.

I ask the naïve question, 'What does a teacher have at her/his disposal in a classroom, with which the achievements of classrooms are created?'. This question helps me focus on the lived practicalities of life in classrooms, but with the particular purpose of learning in mind. Given that the classroom is not ideally designed for learning, this question helps me read more selectively the acres of print devoted to classrooms, putting to one side the prescriptive and to another side the grand narratives which have little link to practical action.

As indicated in Figure 2.1, my answer to this naïve question has been cast in terms of some general overlapping heading each of which has practical importance:

This model has had a good response in publications on mentoring beginner teachers[1] and on managing classroom behaviour.[2] Chapters 5 to 9 will address these areas as they relate to the practices of building learning communities in classrooms.

The telling of stories about teaching offers a means of communicating practice which (i) accommodates the complexity and ambiguity of the context, (ii) enhances teacher's voice and (iii) avoids the 'one-size fits all' stance. It also turns out to be engaging in that it is more likely to lead to dialogue, and influential in that it is more remembered (many of the books which beginner teachers report as influential from their training are first-person accounts of classroom life). It's not the only way to communicate practice, so I will add to some of the stories that are re-told in these chapters frameworks and ideas collected from other accounts. In this way my role will be to offer extra meanings and maintain the big picture.

Practice and vision go together, so the description of classroom practices cannot be divorced from the vision which helps the practice come to life. Equally in order for the vision to be realised we need practical action. On that note, the phrase 'the devil is in the detail' comes to mind, and may well be a useful reminder at times, but I want to propose a more constructive phrase: 'the dream is in the detail'.

Your story so far

In order to promote more engaged reading and to acknowledge your existing experiences, it can be useful to run through the following structure for capturing reflections and achievements. It is also important to identify those elements of a dream which you have experienced already, so that you carry forward into the future the best parts of your past.

Take a few minutes to think of classrooms you have known, and occasions when those classrooms have operated as learning communities. *Choose the best experience you can.* When you have identified that one occasion, do all you can to reconstruct it in your mind's eye – recall the room, the conditions, the people and so on. Capture in concrete detail the things that made that experience possible. Reflect on the following:

- What was working as a learning community?
- How you make sense of this positive occasion.

Try to capture some of what you have identified into a provocative proposition:

- 'Classrooms work best as learning communities when . . . '.

  [A provocative proposition provokes thought and stands in contrast to a soggy proposition; for example, 'Classrooms work best as learning communities when the teacher–pupil relations are good'.]

Having used this activity during workshops, I offer below a selection of the propositions which teachers have created (and roughly categorise them into the themes of the forthcoming chapters):

Classrooms work best as learning communities when:

Goals and plans
- Teachers are intentional in planning and facilitating structure and freedom
- They're fun, different and the personal is planned into the learning

- The responsibility for the learning remains with the learner
- Children own their learning experiences
- The pupils cooperate, understand that everyone has something of value to offer, share a common purpose and work together to achieve it

Teacher's role
- Teachers reach out from their comfort zone
- Teachers embrace pupils and their experience
- Teachers and pupils grow together
- Pupils see teacher as more than facilitator – as person, as story-teller
- We deconstruct existing experiences of non-learning communities
- Teachers sacrifice the apparent constraints

Social structure and climate
- There is psychological safety and a balance of challenge and support
- People feel safe enough to take risks and laugh together
- Everyone feels able to take risks, mistakes are not negatively evaluated

Resources and bridging
- The room is a special space
- Boundaries between in-class and out-of-class break down
- Not confined to four walls

My impression from these contributions has been that many teachers have experienced elements of the dream. That is heartening given the dominant culture. And that more practical detail would be welcome for creating more of that vision. That is the hope for this book.

Where might you start?

It's a reasonable enough question to ask, but there's not a clear answer of the linear sort which says, 'Start here at A and then move to B'. When dealing with complex systems like classrooms, there is more than one starting point and more than one ending point for building learning communities. For that reason, the order of Chapters 5 to 9 is pretty arbitrary (although it may be best to consider goals at some time early on). Don't let this possibly ambiguous answer hold you back, however: the best answer is make sure you start somewhere!

Anticipating what you may meet

Given that the approach to learning and classrooms that this book is developing is not the dominant one in our society at this time, certain things follow which it will be useful to anticipate:

1 As members of this society, we won't always feel easy when working and learning this way.
2 A range of pressures and forces in our society will seem to challenge us in this approach.

Over recent years I have learned (in my own practice and when working with other teachers) that:

1 It is useful to recognise that currently 'Classrooms as Learning Communities' is against the grain of everyday views of learning and teaching. The very phrase 'against the grain' can act as a useful reminder of the fact that our vision is not the dominant one, and that a range of dynamics may ensue, both in ourselves and in others.
2 It is necessary to be strategic in coping with the forces that challenge us. For example, a school with a very rich learning community approach will have to ensure that it also has good data on children's performance, in order to keep the agencies of compliance (Ofsted, LEAs) at bay. Given the research evidence cited in this book, you can have every faith that the short-term agenda of performance will be handled and surpassed, and that you will contribute to the much longer-term vision which is the special contribution of educators. Building learning machines may have seemed appropriate for the twentieth century, but it is increasingly recognised that creating learning communities is important for the twenty-first.

The struggle in our heads

The above points have informed another feature of this book, to be found in the following chapters. When we're working against the grain, and being strategic towards current forces, it's too simple to think 'the enemy is out there'. As people who have grown up in society we have partly been created by it and partly been involved in its re-creation. So we have heard and may have spoken the voices of the dominant model: they are active (if not dominant) in the many voices which live in us as social animals. So when we're developing non-dominant practice, we may have to cope with ourselves! We may find that the small voices inside us seem to stop us moving forward and taking appropriate action towards new practice. I put it this way because numbers of colleagues and teachers who have been making such development report two things happen at once: inspiring results at the same time as continuing to feel that it remains a struggle.

So you will find two features in the chapters that follow:

1   Some 'alerts' which ask you to notice the voices within you as you read, especially those which undercut the message of the text.
2   Some accounts from teachers about how their inspiring and engaging practice continued to feel a struggle (so maybe Nirvana is not going to be obtained just beyond the horizon!).

5 Goals in a learning community

Classrooms with purpose

What are the purposes in a classroom, and what implications do the different possible goals have for crucially connected issues such as agency (that of teachers as well as that of pupils), choice and planning? Many key issues about constructive classrooms and building learning communities start with the issue of purpose. In this chapter the current situation in classrooms will be reviewed, before examining extra elements from the other models of learning.

Testing times

The times we're in now are well illustrated by the comment of Kieran, a year 6 teacher, who said:

> 'Do you know what I've found myself doing of late?
> When pupils ask, "Why are we doing this?"
> I've been replying "Because it's in the SATs"'.
> His sense of surprise at himself was clear as he spoke.

Within Kieran's comment are the elements of the major tensions for teaching in current times: are the tests our educational rationale now? My answer is a clear 'no': they could never adequately represent or capture what a young person can gain from their school days, and they will always underestimate the achievements of pupils, teachers and schools. But what else will we say to the learners in our classrooms?

Yes, the tests exist, but the point is that schools' modal response to them leads to a distortion of the goals, process and relationships of learning. To the point that a strong emphasis on performance actually gets worse performance!

But if teachers know that test results are not their core goals, how is it that teacher behaviour can be so influenced by them? There's nothing intrinsic in the mere existence of national tests which *necessarily* leads to teachers operating classrooms in a more teacher-centred way, focusing on 'coverage' (theirs, not the pupils) and doing all the things that are summarised in the phrase 'teaching to the test' (or the version from the USA, 'test-prep lessons'[1]). In order to explain the phenomenon of 'teaching to the test', we have to recognise a further element in the picture. This is the manner in which teachers have been deemed 'responsible' for pupils' performance in the tests. No longer are the scores on performance tests a (distorted, partial and timed) reflection of pupils' attainment, they are now a reflection on the teacher, or (as in performance tables) of the school! This has been a key element in the version of 'accountability' which was introduced to UK schools in the 1990s, a version more derived from accountancy[2] than from human services. It's with these conditions in place, that the modal effects on teaching happen, as was demonstrated in this account from researchers in New York twenty years ago:[3]

In our interviews with teachers, we have heard over and over how many of them have lost some of their enthusiasm for teaching. Initially excited and motivated to teach, to challenge and motivate the children in their classrooms, they tell of how the external pressures of standardized curricula, competency tests, and other manifestations of a culture obsessed with achievement have robbed them of autonomy and creativity with respect to teaching and had a negative impact on their own interest and effectiveness in the classroom milieu. Their reports of how such factors cause them to be less supportive of the children's autonomy led us to another experiment.

We explored the effects of externally set performance standards on teaching styles. Two groups of subjects were asked to teach students how to solve spatial-relations problems. Both groups of subjects were given the same instructions, except that, for one group, a sentence was added telling them that, as teachers, it was their responsibility to see to it that their students performed up to standards. While this addition might seem subtle, it led to dramatic effects. The 20-minute teaching session was tape-recorded and later analyzed. It revealed that those teachers in the performance standards condition made three times as many utterances and their utterances were more likely to be directing, controlling, and to include words like 'should' and 'must'. In short, the pressure created by mentioning performance standards led the subjects to be much more controlling in the teaching task. And this of course is ironic, because so much research has suggested that the less controlling the teacher, the more likely it is that the students will perform well.

1   *Does this story 'ring bells' for your current experience in teaching?*
2   *What counter-examples do you know, where teachers have managed to maintain a focus on learning, despite the existence of the tests?*
3   *How have they managed to do this?*

In some senses this phenomenon is not completely new: classrooms throughout the twentieth-century have illustrated the tendency towards teacher control, and many images of classrooms in earlier centuries portray it too. Seymour Sarason[4] describes it like this:

> In several elementary school classrooms I arranged for observers to be there from the first day of school to the end of the first month. I was after what I described as the forging of the classroom's 'constitution'. . . . Who wrote the constitution of the classroom? The answer – to which there was no exception – was that the teachers wrote the constitution. They articulated the rules and regulations (frequently post hoc) but provided no rationale. There was absolutely no discussion of the rationale. . . . It never occurred to these teachers, who by conventional standards were very good, that students should be provided with a rationale, which deserved extended discussion, and that students should have an opportunity to voice their opinions. . . . In these matters it was as if the teachers had no respect for the needs and opinions of students. Students were and should be powerless in these matters. Their time would come when they 'grew up'.

These are tough observations: do they accord with your experience? But the point is not to indulge in simple blaming of teachers: Sarason analysed the wider system and concluded that *teachers regard students the way their superiors regard them*, and that is a key issue for present times. It's seen in the phenomenon of **passing on** pressure – I'm under pressure so I'll put you under pressure; I've got targets so I'll give you targets. This phenomenon is now voiced at all levels, for example:

> We're putting the teaching profession under a lot of pressure and we're doing it for a simple reason: there are a lot of people putting us under pressure
>
> (Tony Blair)[5]

Not only does this stance lead to distortion of teaching, it contains in it the potential to get worse. The reason I say this is that if when pressure is first applied it doesn't work, the tendency is to apply more pressure. And to carry on doing more of the same, but trying harder to make it happen faster. This stance is to be found in many government strategies such as the literacy hour, booster classes, summer schools, and so on – if pupils aren't learning to read from current programmes, give them more. This escalation of pressure (which has parallels with the escalation of punishment – 'the beatings will continue until morale improves') is often associated with a shift of language and focus. In the UK today, the official voice speaks in the language of militarism: targets, campaigns, crusades, task forces, etc.

So in current times, the view 'Learning = being taught' has been re-emphasised in many places through the form of testing and the approach to accountability. Perhaps this is exactly what was intended by people like the Chief Inspector of Schools who wrote, 'We re-introduce the traditional teaching of literacy and numeracy into primary schools . . . to restore the true purpose of education based on the transmission of knowledge'.[6]

But this is not the picture everywhere. In different countries, in whole schools and in individual classrooms, there are important exceptions to this picture which operate on more effective views of learning. This includes primary schools in the UK which have been subject to the pressures: successful schools are shown to modify and re-plan 'top-down' strategies to their own vision and context.[7] This book re-tells such stories, but I believe you also know some exceptions to the general picture. Try out this reflection to see what you can glean from the examples you know, no matter how small or how large they may be.

Think of a classroom you know, in which the purposes for learning are not cast in terms of tests, pressure, performance and so on. Choose the best example you can. When you have identified that classroom, do all you can to reconstruct it in your mind's eye – recall the room, its messages, the teacher and their communications and so on. Capture in concrete detail the things which make that version of a classroom possible.

Make some notes and then ask yourself:

- *How are the purposes for learning created in this classroom?*
- *What does the teacher contribute in making this possible?*
- *What do the pupils contribute?*

To reach a better resolution for the classroom we need to move away from 'teachers treat their pupils like their superiors treat them'. This will, among other things, lead to better connections between teachers and pupils. Some critics of classroom life like to say 'pupils are compelled to follow someone else's rules, study someone else's curriculum and submit continually to someone else's evaluation', and they make this into a criticism of teachers. I prefer to say 'and at worst this describes teachers too'. Changing this situation to everyone's advantage requires teachers re-finding their voice,[8] and a repositioning of the various voices on the classroom. Rather than teachers becoming ventriloquists mechanically mouthing words provided by government,[9] they need to revisit and revive their own voice on learning. In that process they will be likely to engage more with the pupils' voice on learning – that's one of the hallmarks of classrooms as learning communities. To achieve this, we need to look at classrooms in detail and this chapter focuses on that core element, the goals of the classroom.

Whose goals in the classroom? The voices in classroom goals

Look at these four purpose statements for an individual's learning in a particular classroom:

- I want you to create a succession of sentences that carry your reader with you.
- I want to know how to write a good letter (and enjoy being with my mates).
- I want you to do well in school.
- Pupils should be taught to choose form and content to suit a particular purpose.

Now you might find the next part easy, but that's the point and it's constructive to consider why it's so easy. Which of these four voices is that of the pupil? Which is that of the parent? Which is the teacher? And which is QCA (KS2 En3 Writing)?

Whatever cues you used, and whatever knowledge you have of the four perspectives, you probably had a clear sense of the way that these short statements reflect different particular positions in the world and the way the world is viewed from each position.[10] You get a sense of the 'speaker's identity' and the intentions associated with it.

The everyday experience of teachers – and of pupils – is to be involved in the interplay of these voices, intentions and identities. How do teachers manage in the middle? The answer is to work explicitly with all of them and work towards a rich dialogue between them. In doing so we move away from the stance where schooling is typically about doing things *to* children, not working *with* them. It is not beyond possibility that pupils could come to understand and operate explicitly with all of the voices.

However, one classroom practice which has become popular in the current context could work against this, if it is used in the dominant fashion. The practice which has recently grown up in classrooms is to put the QCA voice on the classroom wall and call it 'the learning objective'. It's not that at all: it's the *teaching* objective, cast in a particular language (not the teacher's) which seems to suggest that an assessment of product can follow. Various impacts derive from this practice, not the least of which is that pupils get bored with it. Perhaps that is related to the finding that many pupils do not understand what it means. As one developer in this field found, 'Only a small minority of children (mainly above average ability Year 6 children) perceived the sharing of learning intention in relation to their learning'.[11]

This practice can introduce a discordant note into otherwise constructive practice. I recently heard a teacher from a primary school in Buckinghamshire talking about how she was helping her class focus on learning. It was engaging and developmental. Then she described using the formal teaching objective to help review learning, and the story she told was one where the pupils were to learn about lists, with examples which were all about pets. At the end of the lesson the teacher asked what had we been learning: the pupils replied 'about pets' to which the teacher responded 'No, it was about lists'.

Pupils driven to abstraction. In that small moment we have a microcosm of major issues in school goals: working with abstract ideas is one of the goals in school, and is a valuable capacity for any human being. But when it is used to disqualify the concrete experience and talk on which the development of abstraction must be based, you can see the point which is made by those who have studied learning in a range of contexts: schools sometimes seem to *create* failure.[12] It reminds us that the current individualised approach to testable performance in the classroom (which is called a National Curriculum) could well lead to greater polarisation of pupil achievement, rather than the building of effective learning communities.

Some teachers in Kent told me of another effect they had noticed from putting 'learning objectives' on the wall. At the end of lessons when these teachers sometimes had a plenary on 'what we've been learning this lesson', they noticed the pupils reading from the wall! They saw the practice as encouraging pupils to become more strategic and less learning-oriented, and as this was contrary to their goals they discontinued it.

So if used in the dominant fashion, this practice could merely re-emphasise the 'Learning = being taught' model, and in the process silence the various voices identified above. It's a practice from a teacher-centred perspective of classrooms, even though it also manages to silence the particular teacher's voice in a classroom!

Creative teachers improve on this practice, along the lines of the principle mentioned above: to seek a dialogue between the voices. Here are some of the possibilities:

1   Put the QCA-speak on the classroom wall, but then give the class a few minutes in pairs to discuss what they think it could mean. This mediation of the official voice by the members of a class leads to more engagement, and on plenty of occasions a richer sense of purpose than officialdom could have created.

2   After working out what the official voice might mean, learners can then examine which of the things that they want to do that they might be able to do more competently as a result of achieving this. This leads to a more active engagement and connection with their view of their future.

3   Ask learners to tell each other whether they know of any adults who might use the knowledge, understanding or skill which the teaching objective focuses on.

4   Ask learners in a class to communicate some of the above to each other and then start to discuss how they would best go about learning it, helping each other in the process. The furthest reaches of this process would be to ask them to decide how they might know whether someone understood it, and you can bet that they would devise something better than SATs.

Goals and purposes – expanding the possibilities

Discussion of goals and purposes in the classroom often bumps into talk of 'motivation'. It can at times be a hazardous notion, especially when used in its everyday within-person terms: the idea that some people have more of this stuff inside them than do others. The term can also attract a moral quality which casts the other, supposedly unmotivated, person in a deficit mode rather than appreciating their quality. Both of these were summed up by the teacher who I heard said, 'The kids at this school aren't motivated. They just want to climb flagpoles'. Speaking as someone who avoids most masts, I was impressed!

Researchers of motivation soon depart from the everyday notions of motivation, since they do not adequately explain the facts of how we all engage in some things and not others. As leading writers put it, 'motivation exists in the relation between individuals and activities'.[13] How the issue of purpose is handled in that relation has given us the distinction between intrinsic and extrinsic motivation. Intrinsic means doing something for its own sake and the experience it offers: extrinsic means doing something because it leads to a separable outcome (for example, a reward). The evidence from research on this issue is much clearer than most everyday beliefs. Researchers who have examined these issues for two decades conclude:

> Although the issue of rewards has been hotly debated, a recent meta-analysis[14] confirms that virtually every type of expected tangible reward made contingent on task performance does, in fact, undermine intrinsic motivation. Furthermore, not only tangible rewards, but also threats, deadlines, directives, and competition pressure diminish intrinsic motivation because . . . people experience them as controllers of their behavior. On the other hand, choice and the opportunity for self-direction appear to enhance intrinsic motivation, as they afford a greater sense of autonomy.[15]

So the driving implication for classrooms is to promote as much intrinsic motivation as possible. Intrinsic motivation results in high-quality learning and creativity. Steps on this way may be helped by this view that there is more than a polarised distinction between intrinsic and extrinsic. In some conditions someone can make an 'external' goal their own and feel part of it, as illustrated in these six different possible responses to the question 'Why do this homework?':

1 It's not for me		'amotivated'
2 To avoid detention	external	⎤
3 To please my parents	somewhat external	extrinsic
4 To get the GCSEs I want	somewhat internal	motivation
5 Because I want to be successful	internal	⎦
6 Because it's interesting		intrinsic motivation

The nearer we can get to intrinsic motivation the better. Given that motivation is not 'inside' people but in the relations between people and activities, no one activity is indicated for 'creating' intrinsic motivation. In the example of homework, the task would really have to be interesting, which usually means that it holds novelty, challenge or aesthetic value for that individual.

Applying this idea to what is said in the classroom context reminds us of the quote from Kieran which opened this chapter: 'Do it because it's in the SATs'. That was an extrinsic view, and Kieran was surprised at himself as it did not fit with his beliefs about motivation. Using the above dimension we can now locate a wider range of the short statements which relate to classroom purpose; these are laid out in Table 5.1.

The statements in Table 5.1 have been grouped and laid out in this way because (notwithstanding the point that there's a continuum) they speak to me of some important distinctions which may be discerned in the goals of classroom activity. These are shown in Table 5.2.

To operate classrooms as learning communities requires that we work towards the lower two cells in this table. The balance has been towards

Table 5.1 Classroom purpose statements

Do it to avoid detention Do it for me Do it because it's in the exam	Do it to avoid social exclusion Do it to please your parents Do it for the school Do it for your success in later life
Do it to succeed Do it because it's interesting Do it because you'll learn Do it to contribute to all our learning Do it to improve knowledge	Do it because you can use it Do it to find out what that world is like Do it to make a difference to the world

Table 5.2 Classroom goal possibilities

Goals which are:	
Internal to the classroom, but external to the learner	External to the classroom, and external to the learner
Internal to the classroom, and internal to the learner	External to the classroom, but internal to the learner

the upper two, and the dialogue is one part of shifting the balance. In achieving this we may recognise many forces which work against it, but it is crucial to note that teachers' knowledge and beliefs about motivation are not one of them. Even though the action patterns of the modal classroom may be veering towards the extrinsic, this is not to be simply explained as teachers wishing it that way. Research on teachers' beliefs about strategies for motivating learners indicates that these beliefs are broadly consonant with the evidence that has emerged from research on motivation, including that mentioned above.[16] But in this sort of research the focus is on how an individual teacher can 'motivate' an individual pupil. This may be important, but it can't be the whole picture since it misses out the wider context and social relations of the classroom.

In order to move on from the teacher-centred view and 'Learning = being taught', we can explore practices which come from the next model of learning, 'Learning = individual sense-making'. The two themes which follow, choosing to learn and planning to learn, have been researched within this model under such terms as self-determination[17] and self-regulation.[18] These are also key elements in the idea of agency which was proposed in Chapter 3 as a hallmark of community, so we will also be moving towards considering classroom purposes in a community.

Choosing to learn

Pupils may seem to make few choices in their classrooms and learning, but many teachers I meet recognise that too many of them might really be making another choice:

> Students in all classrooms have always had the power to make the most basic choice about their learning: they may choose to engage in learning or to disengage. We cannot remove that choice. Our goal is to inspire students to choose to engage. When they do, we know that they can and will make good choices about what they learn and how they assess their learning.[19]

From this stance it is possible to consider how pupils might make classroom choices on:

- what they learn;
- how they learn;
- how well they learn;
- why they learn.

And on each of these dimensions there could be more or less significant choices made. One of the most comprehensive examples is given in the story of Susan Moon:

Susan is a teacher of English and Spanish. She is with her class of 13-year-olds. On the board are the mandated curriculum requirements for the subject: Susan is standing beside a flipchart.

The class had been through this process before, so they are prepared. 'Okay,' Susan says, 'this is what we have to demonstrate that we know. Any ideas how we are going to do that?'

With almost no lapse, the pupils begin to propose ideas and argue the merits of each until they identify a project they believe would permit each student to meet the requirements. Once Susan feels confident that their choices would allow them to do well, she asks 'Okay, you're going to need money to do this – how are you going to get it?' Once again the pupils address the question with energy.

When interviewed some time later, Susan explained that she had made some leaps of faith – that the pupils could learn basic Spanish skills by following the plan they had devised: planning lessons and teaching Spanish to younger students. It felt risky, and she worried all year long.

As her colleague teaching the other Spanish class finished chapter after chapter in the Spanish textbook, her anxiety grew.

At the end of the year, the kids took the mandated tests. They scored the highest for her region in the first part, and second highest in the second part.

Despite the success Susan was still subject to the lingering suspicion that Spanish should be learned by covering chapters.

As you read this account, can you notice the voices inside you? Were they anything like:

- That's a bit far-fetched (it can't happen here).
- I wonder where that was (it can only happen there).
- I bet the kids were special (ordinary kids couldn't act like that).
- I expect it's something you can do with Spanish (but not with my subject) and others.

These are examples of the voices of disqualification, attempting to downplay the message and possible impact of the story. Could we bring on any other voices? Anything like:

- That makes sense (and if Susan can do it, why not me?).
- I could try something out (best to start with a small experiment).
- Perhaps I could do it with my [X] class (best to prepare them a bit).

Monitor how the balance of voices goes with you, and see which pathway you take.

Susan's story is especially important because it took place in a context of mandated testing. It also highlights one of the things to anticipate when making change: the ongoing sense of slight unease that a teacher can feel as they develop non-modal practices which are obviously successful. But it is a fully-developed example on a number of levels of learner choice, and we don't need to change everything at once! So let's consider further possibilities on a lesser scale, in order to entertain an experiment or two in classrooms we know (at the same time giving less room for those voices of disqualification).

Choices in what to learn

This can range from choosing which of a set of problems to begin with, where in a given text to start reading, which story for the class to have to read at the end of the day, and so on. Each time a choice is made, engagement is likely to increase, and learners set themselves a level of challenge which works for them.

Choices in how to learn

This might begin with which reading place to choose, whether to present a recently-written account, whose questions to take on it, and so on. It could include and develop towards whether to work alone, in small groups or as a class.[20]

Choices in how well to learn

The criteria through which any product is judged are less motivating if they remain someone else's criteria. Choosing how best to demonstrate understanding, and devising questions to check understanding leads to depth and challenge. It also gives students more control, makes evaluation feel less punitive, and provides an important learning experience in itself. If pupils can create a complex question to assess understanding of something, the need for testing it reduces greatly!

Choices in why to learn

Discussions of purpose are rare in our classrooms, yet underneath pupils are already making choices. Some are resolving to 'Do it to please their parents' while others will be operating some version of 'Do it to avoid detention'. Bringing these into the open and discussing many of the statements in Table 5.1 will bring other purposes into the discourse and help learners try out new purposes of their own.[21]

Voices against choice

Some of the reasons given for keeping pupils in such a low-agency role have been rehearsed for generations. This is what makes them conservative, and sometimes difficult to counter as we hear them in ourselves. I include a selection below, and (in the tradition of the understanding that every utterance includes an invitation to another voice) I attach the responses I felt myself making to each.

'Kids can't have absolute freedom'.

> Where did that extreme suggestion come from? Must be some emotion floating around in this debate. No one is proposing 'unfettered' choice: that would not be developmental and definitely not realistic.

'They're not mature enough yet'.

> So how long will we wait? And in the meantime why aren't we helping them mature?

'It takes too long'.

> But this is time well spent if they really are learning to make responsible decisions and in the process increase their engagement.

'Children need limits'.

> Everyone has constraints – that's one of the things we learn when making choices – but there's no need to create artificial limits. Classrooms are artificial enough already!

'What about the needs of others in the class?'

> Good point, and exactly the point for classrooms as learning communities: sometimes pupils will be called upon to make genuine choices which implicate one of their colleagues' learning needs, like 'how will you make sure you've prepared your contribution to the group?' and 'how will you help others to learn?'

Planning to learn

Pupil planning has a significant effect on learning and achievement. One study of GCSE results showed that the scores of pupils who plan least are just 30 per cent of the scores of pupils who plan most. And this was not a reflection of some fixed capacity 'inside' individual learners: the context was influential in that there was a higher percentage of motivated pupils in schools adopting a collaborative approach than in those characterised as adopting an interventionist approach.[22]

The change which can be brought about by encouraging pupils to plan their approach to activities is significant. It contributes to the development of more self-directed learners. But that phrase is open to various interpretations, depending on the view of learning which is adopted. The three possibilities outlined below give a sense of how the degree of purpose which learners exercise and the extent of planning they undertake is strongly linked to the view of learning.

From the stance 'Learning = being taught', a self-directed learner is seen to:

- focus on a given activity;
- manage distractions;
- organise information they are given;
- focus on the teacher and what they are saying.

But this is all from a compliance view of learning

From the stance 'Learning = individual sense-making', a self-directed learner is seen to:

- generate their own enquiries;
- plan how they'll go about an activity (including activities such as reading and writing);
- monitor how well an activity is going;
- review whether the strategies they have used have proved effective.

As these two 11-year-olds put it:
'When I'm stuck, I go back and check instead of guessing' (Vikcsh).
'I am good at finding short cuts and providing tactical tips' (Daniel).

From the stance 'Learning = building knowledge with others', a self-directed learner is seen to:

- select from their environment appropriate resources they need for learning (peers, teachers, other resources);
- generate with others motivation and goals;
- promote and develop with others dialogue for learning;
- interrelate learning from various contexts of their learning landscape.

Such capacities develop through the promotion of classrooms as learning communities.

The greater opportunity and range for planning that pupils have the more they will develop a sense of urgency as a learner. Should you wish to enquire about these matters with learners, Table 5.3 shows a framework of items which asks them about planning strategy, managing

Table 5.3 Framework for enquiry into pupils' 'feeling in charge of learning'

We're interested in your views about your learning.

There aren't any 'right' or 'wrong' answers.

Can you tell us how much you feel you're in charge of your learning?

Just put a tick in the column on the right, to show whether you:

SA: agree a lot;   A: agree;   D: disagree;   SD: disagree a lot

	SA	A	D	SD
1 Before I start my classwork I work out the best way to do it				
2 I can do my best even if I don't like what the lesson is about				
3 When my teacher gives hints on how best to do something I'll try them out				
4 I sometimes ask myself 'Am I going about this the best way?'				
5 I know when I've understood something when I can say it in my own words				
6 If I find something difficult in class, I talk to the teacher				
7 I don't ask questions in class				
8 When I'm reading I sometimes stop to make sure I'm understanding				
9 With a new topic I can usually find something interesting to learn				
10 When I get new classwork I jump straight in and sometimes wish I hadn't				
11 When I don't understand something in a lesson, I ask a classmate				

From: . . . . (Name)   . . . . (Tutor group)

motivation, using strategies, monitoring strategies, monitoring understanding, and using people in their environment,

The framework shown in Table 5.3 is best used to promote discussion
among learners. But for understanding a group of pupils and for monitoring how well their environment promotes them feeling in charge,
scores can be created. If you allocate $-2, -1, +1, +2$ to the four responses
(reversing the direction for items 7 and 10) possible scores range from
-22 to $+22$. In the responses I have collected from 600 11-year-olds, the
actual scores have ranged from -14 to $+20$. Since high scores denote a
strong sense of being in charge of one's own learning, through planning,
using and monitoring strategies and making good use of other people,
there are clearly some constructive learners and some causes for
concern.

The final item in that framework raises the issue of learners helping
each other and therefore the wider social relations in the classroom.
Before we leave the theme of planning, our transition should also note
that even in times of mandated testing, teachers can forge the possibilities for planning with pupils, including some joint planning on the
learning approaches which would best meet their goals.[23]

Motivation is social, learning is social

Many of young people's most important goals are social:

> we found that students list many socio-emotional goals among
> their most salient personal goals, such as being respected, being
> supportive, sticking to an agreement, being treated fairly, having
> harmonious contacts with peers, maintaining confidence in public,
> and getting valued for effort. These goals were salient in and out
> of school. Surprisingly, two interpersonal goals, namely 'be ready
> to help anyone' and 'have harmonious contacts with peers' were
> considered more valuable in an out-of-school context than at
> school. This finding suggests that teachers have not been successful
> in making schools places where young people infuse academic goals
> with social value.[24]

In addressing the theme of 'motivation is social', some writers and
researchers have added social goals to the list of goals they focus on, but
this remains an individual model. A further step is to recognise that

individual motivation of whatever sort is for social purposes. Ask a very simple, basic question – 'Why does anyone do anything?' – and you soon have to recognise the importance of how the person views themselves, who they want to become, their meaningful world and so on. In particular, their future selves inform much of their action and feeling.[25] Context is influential in all this, including the cultural messages, whether these be towards self-enhancement as in the USA, or self-criticism as in Japan.[26] This also reflects wider cultural trends in the balance of valuing independence or interdependence, even though much research on motivation has assumed the former.[27]

So just imagine what the possibilities are if classrooms and schools were to engage social dimensions of motivation more fully, instead of relegating the social to the cause of difficulties. An example of that latter point is when (more so in secondary schools) pupils' peers are talked about as a negative influence – folk theories of 'peer pressure' are invoked, as though they were indicative of the age. By contrast, some evidence I have gathered from 600 pupils about what helps them feel part of secondary school shows that friends are mentioned a great deal and that they are mentioned as a helpful influence.

Another step in viewing motivation as social is to recognise that individual identities and advancements are always community-related. The potentially individualistic 'who I want to be' always implies becoming part of something, usually a community of people involved in an activity through a range of roles and contributions. Action is always social: so also is the inclination to act.

The classroom application of this is found in those settings where teachers and pupils operate together and learn the identities which accompany membership of particular knowledge communities, as in 'Let's be scientists', 'Let's be poster writers', or French-speakers, mathematicians, researchers, music-makers and so on.

Human learning is necessarily and fundamentally social: it utilises language, culture and communication, and implicates our identities and preferred futures. All of these are social creations and are being dynamically re-created. We build our identities and connections around our work, knowledge and contributions to our communities. Yet, sadly, schools often behave as if the social were a threat to learning, or think it should be addressed in a low-status corner of the curriculum.

The challenge to make this our direction is well put:

No amount of change in schools will produce significant results unless the nature of school as a social entity is taken seriously.

No amount of clever delivery of subject matter will capture the imaginations and energies of students who feel that their opportunities for social development lie elsewhere.[28]

Community goals

Here, as in earlier chapters, it is useful to beware weak versions of what we are addressing. For example, descriptions of the process of getting a team or a class to develop collective goals often use terms like 'shared goals'. What does this mean? What happens if members of a collective 'share' goals? Do they merely tell each other what goals each has? Is that sharing? Or do they do that and seek commonalities? Similarly with 'common goals': what could this mean? Is it that a single goal has been taken to stand for everyone? If so, how has this happened? Has diversity been squashed and (as is often the case) some version of power used to create uniformity? To me these are weak versions, not only because the detail of their process invites scepticism, but also because they are more about the communication of individual members' goals rather than forging a goal for the collective.

The goal of a learning community is to enhance the learning of all its members – in relation to the topics in hand as well as the ways of going about them, including the process of the community. With this starting point we can now imagine a different set of goal statements in a classroom, such as:

In this classroom:

- Our goal is to create a learning community.
- Our goal is to improve knowledge together – of this topic and of how best to learn.
- Our goal is to learn together as best we can.
- Our goal is to help each other learn.
- Our goal is to learn how to learn together.

If you imagine a teacher starting to voice these goals for a classroom, you might also imagine that such phrases may feel unusual at first. I still experience some of this strangeness. It reflects the socialisation we have experienced, and many learners recognise this explicitly. They also take a while to develop their own version of the practices which follow, and may ask a lot of questions about how it could happen rather than trying to make it happen.

The development of these goals in practice takes a journey of experiencing, reviewing, learning and publicising. Juliet's class of 10-year-olds had spent some time discussing their experience of learning: when it was best, what helped and so on, and then developed the emerging stance for their classroom into a set of principles:

Agreed principles for a learning environment in 6B

1 We need to listen to each other.
2 We need varied, challenging and enjoyable learning experiences and opportunities.
3 We need to maintain an appropriate noise level.
4 We need to respect each others' feelings, ideas, interests and beliefs.
5 We need to arrive at school ready to learn, having eaten and slept well.
6 We need to focus on one learning objective in turn.
7 We need to cooperate, sharing our thoughts, ideas, understandings, concerns, difficulties and opinions.

After some time operating with these ideas, the class reviewed their principles and added the following:

---

8 We need to have the confidence to make mistakes.
9 We need to question what we are told or what seems obvious or correct.
10 We need to feel that we have an equal chance to contribute/ speak.

Many things strike me about these principles, which were displayed on the wall near the classroom door, signed by all the class, and with a very interesting message saying that 6B wished these for their visitors too:

- They are phrased as 'we' (in contrast to many of the 'codes' or worse which one can find on classroom walls).
- They set the scene for, and indeed develop, rich ideas about learning (in contrast to those which omit learning and thus seem to emphasise behavioural compliance).
- They increasingly emphasise the role of social processes in learning.

Whichever way that community goals are developed and made public, in the end it is the lived experience which convinces learners that this is a beneficial way to operate, and for many transforms their view of themselves in relation to others and learning. Here are the voices of some teachers at the end of a ten-week course:

- 'I now know what that phrase "the social nature of knowledge" means. It was a phrase in texts – now it's a lived experience'.
- 'I am no longer alone in my thoughts'.
- 'When I started on this module I wanted ten things I could do to make me a better teacher. Now I know that's not it. I see relationships as central and I listen to relationships better in my classroom now'.
- 'I used to believe that I learnt from more experienced and well-read professors or lecturers. I did not believe that I could learn from a peer or colleague in my group'.
- 'Being able to learn with others has helped me to understand about how learning can be constructed through social participation. Sharing ideas, opinions, doubts and questions in an atmosphere of trust increases understanding and builds confidence to investigate problems and misconceptions together'.
- 'We build more together than we could build on our own'.
- 'I have realised that my initial frustrations at the concept of a community assessment were unfounded, and that actually a community assessment embodies our community aim and our purpose of learning'.

- 'The strongest feeling I had at the close of our learning community was a feeling of great success and that what I had experienced was one of the most positive learning experiences I have had. I thought back to the first day of the module and how I had been so sure I was not going to enjoy or benefit from the experience and I was incredibly glad that I did not leave'.
- 'It was an unforgettable experience'.

This chapter does not end with a fixed set of guidelines for action, because that would not reflect the way classrooms are or the way learning happens. But some principles for discussing and extending purpose have emerged, and these do offer some indications for action. Goals and purposes are not the whole picture of classroom life but they serve to take us to the next theme: tasks in a classroom as a learning community. And perhaps the two main themes to carry over to that chapter are the need for purposeful tasks and for learning about learning.

Prompts for reflection

- Can you apply the framework in Figure 5.2 to review the profile of goal statements you currently use in your classroom?
- Review the choices which pupils make in your classroom, especially those which are choices regarding learning. Does the current picture invite further development? What ideas for their choices in learning have occurred to you?
- When are pupils asked to plan something about their learning in your classroom? Could there be more such occasions?
- Can you draft some ideas for how to phrase some appropriate community goals for your classroom? How would you best engage the pupils' voice in developing this?

6 Tasks in a learning community

Creating knowledge together

In any classroom the tasks being progressed have a defining effect on the nature of classroom life and learning. They can impact on engagement or drift, challenge or boredom, and feelings of competence or failure. Teachers' everyday thinking reflects the core role of tasks when they ask, 'What shall I get them to do this lesson?'. Similarly, research into classroom management helps us see the task of the teacher as managing the engagement of pupils in productive activities for the allocated time, and that teachers actually manage activities rather than students. One implication of this is well put in Walter Doyle's conclusion: 'if an activity system is not established and running in a classroom, no amount of discipline will create order'.[1]

So what are the characteristics of classroom tasks which contribute to building a learning community? And what guiding lights are there to help us construct such tasks in our own classrooms?

The structure of this chapter is to build up an answer from starting with current patterns of practice, adding dimensions as we go. The reasons for doing it this way are twofold: first so that the classroom as a learning community doesn't seem like some impossible other world but is one that can be incrementally built, and second so that we recognise the forces currently at work and the limitations they create. Strictly speaking, we are not 'adding' dimensions because they are there all the time, but we are incorporating more dimensions into the design of tasks.

Schemes of work, or schemes of learning?

Since the introduction of the so-called 'National Curriculum' in England there has been a steady increase in the specification of classroom tasks coming from central sources. Most recently the government's 'National Literacy Strategy' and the 'National Numeracy Strategy' have taken this trend to an even greater degree of specification, adding timings, sequences and even scripts for teachers. There might be little difficulty with such specification if it supported really rich learning, but my view is that it does the opposite, focusing on short-term performance notions and actually doing damage to pupils' development of longer-term learning capacities. This National Curriculum is founded on deep-seated yet unexamined cultural beliefs about teaching leading to learning: this is indicated by its heading every page with 'Pupils will be taught that . . . '. The revised version (2000) simply substitutes that phrase with 'Pupils should learn to . . . ' but the content and style of specification remain the same!

A particular indication of the stance on learning is to be found in those documents which are now called 'Schemes of Work'. The title is of course a give-away for the sort of classroom culture and classroom discourse it creates – a discourse of work as opposed to a discourse of learning, as discussed in Chapter 2. Up until two or three years ago, it was possible to be reasonably relaxed about schemes of work, since they were written in schools and varied in important ways between schools. I remember one occasion of asking twenty secondary school science mentors to bring in their schemes of work to our mentoring course: the initial purpose was to examine how they could support beginner teachers being creative and going beyond these specifications. But the unplanned learning was of greater impact: there was so much variation between these documents and their underlying view of teaching and learning that participants soon questioned the official rhetoric which portrays all schools as doing the same National Curriculum.

Times have changed again, and now there are schemes of work available centrally from the DfES, easily downloadable from its website. The enormous significance of this has escaped many people and not been sufficiently critiqued. The significance would not have escaped one of England's foremost thinkers of the last century, Bertrand Russell. In 1930,[2] his experience of the USA led him to foresee a connection between mechanised production and schooling:

> Production is cheaper when it is unified and on a large scale than when it is divided into a number of small units. This applies quite as much to the production of opinions as the production of pins. The principal sources of opinion in the present day are the schools, the Churches, the Press, the cinema, and the radio. The teaching in the elementary schools must inevitably become more and more standardised as more use is made of apparatus. It may, I think, be assumed that both the cinema and the radio will play a rapidly increasing part in school education in the near future. This will mean that the lessons will be produced at a centre and will be precisely the same wherever the material prepared at this centre is used.

Although he foresaw the process of standardisation, Russell in 1930 could not have anticipated the vehicle of the Internet or that by 2000 the agents of this process would be the state.

Another 'give-away' on the DfES website for schemes of work is the statement that they have not been created for English or Maths. Thus the government's 'National Literacy Strategy' and 'National Numeracy Strategy' have taken over the central prescription for what were previously seen as core subjects. It is likely that this was the only method government could employ for increased prescription, side-stepping as it does those few but important clauses in the National Curriculum legislation which maintained the professional role of teachers in deciding such detail.[3]

But no matter how this state of affairs has come about, its impact on learning should be our biggest concern. Here the schemes of work exhibit key pointers. Through the specification of 'learning objectives' (i.e. the official voice on teaching purposes as discussed in the previous chapter) and also specifying 'learning outcomes', learning is reduced to the tangible and short-term. The first example from the new Citizenship schemes of work for Key Stages 1 and 2 (Unit 1: 'Taking Part: developing skills of communication and participation') tells us:

Learning objective
Children should learn to understand what is involved in effective listening.

Learning outcome
Children describe what effective listening involves.

What? Notwithstanding the considerations of Chapter 5 in terms of whose voice says that pupils need to learn such things as 'effective listening' (and the deficit view of children implied in this example), why should children **describe** what effective listening involves, instead of enacting it in their classroom life? This is a good example of what limited views schemes of work can create, with a premium on simple assessment of the tangible. The way that the so-called outcome has been constructed provides a good example of 'procedural display',[4] and is a reflection of the instructional conception of learning: I teach you, You learn, You show me.

Sometimes the difference between objective and outcome is trivial. The next example in the same scheme of work states:

Learning objective
Children should learn to take turns in discussion and take different views into account.

Learning outcome
Children take turns in discussion and take different views into account.

The trivialisation in such prescriptions can sadly extend to how the content is perceived on matters which could be important in children's lives:

Learning objective
Children should learn to develop their understanding of the difference between right and wrong.

Learning outcome
Children should understand the difference between right and wrong.

This example shows how such specification narrows our view of outcomes: when measurable performances are the aim, compliance is encouraged. Discussion of right and wrong, and discussion of the more common difficulty of having to choose between two 'rights', is simply turned into 'understanding the difference' – some sort of depersonalised understanding which of course we can expect all teachers to hold.

I do hope that if your professional life is impacted on by schemes of work they are richer than the examples above. But how can a classroom teacher improve on the limitations of the official voice, and create something richer. Indeed, how may we move from schemes of work to schemes of learning?

Extending the range of tasks

The range of tasks in the modal classroom is still skewed in a direction which has been known for hundreds of years. A reflection of this is given by the cumulative data which Mike Hughes[5] has collected from hundreds of secondary school pupils. They report that the most frequent activities in classrooms are:

1   listening;
2   answering questions from a book;
3   teachers' questions; and
4   taking notes.

I imagine that all of those are familiar to you! They would have been familiar to Victorian schoolchildren, and even to the children in the classroom of 1658 shown in Figure 6.1.

Figure 6.1 Classroom image from the first children's textbook, 1658

Source: John Amos Comenius (1658) *Orbis Sensualium Pictus*. Facsimile of 1672 English edition from the collection of Professor Ayers Bagley

Moving on from such established patterns is not always simple, but the need to do so is poignantly put by two year 10 students talking to Caroline Lodge about the lessons they would like:

Gill: 'When you can get up and do things . . . instead of just me and my work.'

Darren: 'Yes, just you, a pen and a piece of paper.'

As a stimulus to extending from the time-honoured range, take a look at the array of words in Figure 6.2, all of which could describe possible classroom tasks. As you scan across these words, do some feel more familiar than others? And of those which are less familiar, is there anything you notice about them, any way in which they seem similar?

Perhaps some of the words which have high 'cognitive' emphasis are less familiar. For example: 'classify', 'analyse' and 'synthesise'. Certainly these do not get emphasised in the dominant conception of learning as instruction. But they are a feature of classrooms in which a conception of learning as sense-making is being developed.[6] Some of these words

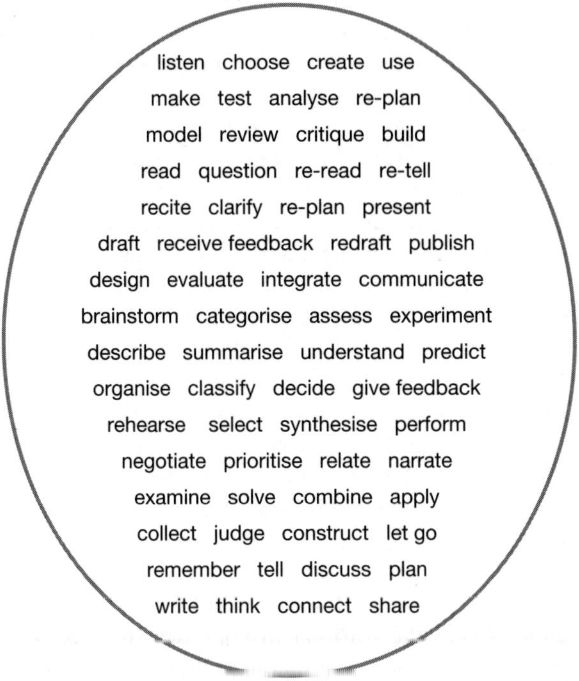

listen   choose   create   use
make   test   analyse   re-plan
model   review   critique   build
read   question   re-read   re-tell
recite   clarify   re-plan   present
draft   receive feedback   redraft   publish
design   evaluate   integrate   communicate
brainstorm   categorise   assess   experiment
describe   summarise   understand   predict
organise   classify   decide   give feedback
rehearse   select   synthesise   perform
negotiate   prioritise   relate   narrate
examine   solve   combine   apply
collect   judge   construct   let go
remember   tell   discuss   plan
write   think   connect   share

Figure 6.2 An array of words for tasks in learning

are phrased in high-level form which, if children are not used to them, will take a little getting used to, but do not assume that this would be impossible. From ages 3 to 8, children are talking meaningfully and consistently about 'thinking' and 'knowing' and other mental states, about 3 per cent of the time.[7] We must make sure that in the classrooms they enter there is at least this amount of focus in the tasks on offer. That way we might reduce replications of the scenario in which a 6-year-old handing in an assignment said to her teacher: 'I did it, but I don't know what it means'.[8]

Tasks for learning

Although the phrase is used frequently, it is a misrepresentation to say 'We learn by doing'. There are plenty of examples of human beings doing the same thing time and again and *not* learning, so it is better to conclude that doing is a necessary but not sufficient element in learning. This means that we need to specify the link between doing and learning, and the question of how do we learn from experience becomes useful. Here the key point is: 'It is not sufficient simply to have an experience in order to learn. Without reflecting upon this experience it may quickly be forgotten or its learning potential lost'.[9]

A useful model for the process of learning from experience is given in Figure 6.3.[10] This cycle highlights activity in learning (Do), the need for reflection and evaluation (Review), the extraction of meaning from the review (Learn), and the planned use of learning in future action (Apply). Perhaps the challenge for all of us is to devise the classroom tasks which promote this cycle of meaningful learning.

If you now look back at the array of words, each line was written with four possible tasks, and I tried to capture (in a fairly rough-and-ready way) a sense of Do → Review → Learn → Apply in each line. Does that sense come across? You probably have your own experiences with other examples of sequences of tasks that have promoted meaningful learning. Recall those occasions and consider whether the tasks compared in some way to the Do → Review → Learn → Apply cycle.

My guess is that the learning in your example showed another important feature: it was 'compositional'. You and the others involved did not know what the end-point would be, but it emerged as the process went on. That's an important aspect of rich learning – you couldn't have

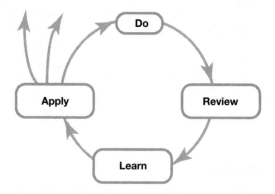

Figure 6.3 A model of the process of learning

predicted it at the outset (let alone planned it). In this way it contrasts with the dominant focus on performance which is present in official pronouncements.

I also imagine that your examples were 'consequential': the learners involved felt that they could do something differently as a result of the learning. As discussed in the previous chapter, this is essential for really high levels of engagement in the classroom, so perhaps your examples were ones where the goals and purposes of the tasks had conveyed this well. This point makes an important contribution to current concerns about learners disengaging from classrooms in the UK, especially towards the end of primary school. A similar phenomenon in US schools is called 'fourth grade slump' and is associated with teaching isolated skills for state tests. A longitudinal study with 431 pupils showed that they become less learning-oriented and more work avoidant from Grade 3.[11] In this context they found that reading and writing tasks which are challenging, collaborative and multi-day reversed the trend, especially with low-achieving pupils. These 9-year-olds preferred high-challenge tasks requiring longer writing, collaboration and extending over more than one school day in contrast to tasks which were short, completed alone and lasting a single lesson. Preferred examples included essays on own choice of topic, letters to politicians, research papers, and letters to next year's class, and contrasted with non-preferred examples of worksheets on vowels, pronouns and vocabulary, spelling and handwriting exercises. They view the latter as boring and requiring minimal thought.[12] High-challenge tasks were preferred because of aspects of the learning process: pupils felt creative, experienced positive emotions and worked hard.

This research reminds me of a story told to me by a headteacher of a primary school in Brent. A decision had been made to leave some classrooms open at break-time, including one of the rooms equipped with computers. While touring the rooms one day she saw Brian fully engaged at a keyboard. He seemed to be using e-mail, and when she checked he was. Brian was happy to help the headteacher out with some of the things she was finding difficult about e-mail, and then she asked him what he found it useful for:

Brian: 'I've been writing to local councillors and the MP and Ken Livingstone 'cos I didn't get my first choice of secondary school.'

Head: 'And what do you find?'
Brian: 'I find it's more successful than letters – you're more likely to get a reply'.
Head: 'You've written letters too?'
Brian: 'Yes'.

In telling the story, the headteacher conveyed her amazement at Brian being so active, but she had also learned about the power of purpose when it comes to writing.

The importance of challenge can also be forgotten in the over-prescribed over-planned performance-oriented classroom, with negative impact on learning and performance. 'Moderate challenge . . . is essential for maximising learning . . . and intellectual development'.[13] So we should be teaching 'students to tolerate failure for the sake of true success' and ' . . . to reach beyond their intellectual grasp'. A study of 10- to 12-year-olds[14] showed that their risk-taking habits could be influenced in the classroom, making the difference between them choosing more difficult problems to solve or choosing tasks far below their achievement levels.

When tasks and their associated goals have been sufficiently worked through and high engagement in the learning process follows, the final parts of the learning cycle have a significant impact in keeping a good process going. When learners of all sorts know that they can do something different in their world as a result of their learning, then there is little difficulty in moving from new meaning to new action (the 'Apply' phase). This stands in contrast to the sort of classrooms where tasks have little consequence, and that idea of 'procedural display' returns as a much more limited goal, the sort which is a candidate for easy assessment.

In the view of learning as construction, as supported by the learning cycle above, the tasks for assessing learning would be significantly different, because what learning is taken to mean is different. When learning is a process of making meaning, tangible displays are less appropriate than other ways which make the meaning-making visible. A range of practices is possible:

- making reasoning public;
- thinking aloud together;

- explaining to one another;
- dialoguing for new ideas;
- giving a reflective commentary;
- thought-experiments.

What is advantageous about these practices is that they are part of good classroom processes for promoting learning, rather than an add-on. And further, although I have introduced them at this point as assessment tasks, there is plenty of evidence that when these processes frequent classroom life, not only is there a clearer indication of the process of meaning-making but also results on performance tests improve.

Here it is useful to note that most of these are ways of making *individual* learning visible, and that they depend on verbal interaction (and gleaning something from it). So they fall mainly in the individual sense-making view of learning. But the fact that all of them need other partners for discussion and dialogue is indicating the next, crucial, step in designing tasks for classrooms as learning communities: they need to be explicitly social.

Tasks for meta-learning

The incidence of learning about learning in our classrooms is quite limited, yet the tasks which promote it are quite straightforward. The difference between the two may be explained by the history, dominant style and norms of classrooms, rather than by any difficulty inherent in learning about learning. I have also found that learning about learning requires no special language or abstruse concepts which might mystify rather than illuminate. At heart it is the process of talking about one's experience, but this time one's experience of learning. So if learning is the processing of experience to create knowledge, meta-learning is the processing of one's experience of learning to create knowledge.

The classroom tasks and practices are these:

1   *Making learning an object of attention.* This is fundamental, yet I have known people say that they went through their whole school career without noticing a thing about their learning. To attend to one's learning one needs to occasionally *stop the flow* to notice, and cumulatively build up a language for noticing more. Prompts such as

What do we mean by learning? When is it best? Where is it best? What helps? What steps or actions do you take? How does it feel? What surprises have you found? can help people bring attention to their experience of learning. It may be slow to begin but accumulates rapidly.

2   *Making learning an object of conversation.* This soon develops from prompts, and encourages learners to tell and re-tell stories of learning with others leading to dialogue. Further prompts may help: *Tell me about a really good learning experience, what made it so good? What did you contribute?* It also leads to enquiries into learning: *When am I engaged most? What helps? How do I help myself become engaged?*

3   *Making learning an object of reflection.* Reflection helps to develop distance from the immediate experience, to rise above it and make wider meaning, see wider patterns. Writing in a notebook dedicated to the experience of learning – a 'learning log' or 'learning journal' – can help significantly. As one 10-year-old put it, 'As I write I notice and understand more too'.

4   *Making learning an object of learning.* This means being able to explicitly experiment with one's own learning and is a part of becoming more self-directing in learning. The hallmarks of choice and self-direction are involved. *How can you plan to go about your learning? How can you monitor how your learning is going? How can you review how your learning has gone? How will you know that it has been as good as you can get it?*

We may think about meta-learning as an additional cycle in the learning process, as indicated in Figure 6.4. These practices are shown to enhance individual performance.[15] They require open task structures, with choice and self-control. Such tasks in the literacy activities in twelve classrooms also helped 6-year-olds develop intrinsic motivation, metacognition and strategic behaviour.[16] Similarly, writing activities in classrooms supporting self-regulated learning helped 7- and 8-year-olds monitor and evaluate their writing in productive ways, use peers effectively and see teachers as collaborators.[17]

Current practice in English and Irish classrooms suggests there is some way to go in meta-learning. Only a minority of teachers provided opportunities for students to develop metacognitive awareness and strategies about the task of reading in twelve classrooms of 9-year-olds in Leeds and Dublin. These teachers helped learners become more aware of how they learn and acquire or refine strategies for the learning

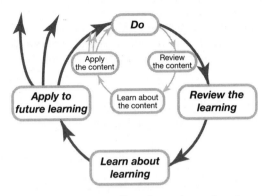

Figure 6.4 A model of the process of learning and meta-learning

of reading: for example, thinking out loud and suggesting ways of tackling a task. They elicited children's prior knowledge and helped them verbalise their experiences, offered guidance on strategies, etc. The other teachers placed great emphasis on the task to be completed, the end product of the activity, pupil compliance with teacher directives, and so on. The promotion of learning strategies and learning about learning was not a prominent feature of classroom life.[18]

Managing tasks for learning

Implications for managing the learning cycle should be considered. In some classrooms I know the model of Do → Review → Learn → Apply is displayed on the wall. I have found that pupils sometimes find it quite straightforward to report on the stage they are at in the cycle. Sometimes teachers find it less easy, but that only reflects to me that the teacher's attention is often in another place to that of the pupils, and in this case it is only the pupils who have immediate access to their own experience. But to the extent that the teacher is managing the learning in a classroom, they have a role in managing the movement through the stages. This is not always as easy as it sounds (and perhaps here is another element in explaining why classrooms retain their traditional patterns). Classrooms often develop a momentum which seems all of their own, and we teachers sometimes find it difficult to stop the flow of pupil activity for the purpose of noticing something important and learning from it (we find it less difficult when it's part of our plan, or when an individual is doing something we don't want). In a conversation on stopping the flow to reflect on learning, Vanessa, a secondary school teacher of drama, strongly identified with this problem in her lessons:

> 'When the group is working on a performance, it's really difficult to get them to stop and examine the detail of what's working well'.
>
> 'So how do you get yourself to do it? Is there anything you say to yourself which helps?'
>
> 'I guess I say to myself that we can't carry on like this'.

It's that stance that our classrooms can be better which leads to fruitful experiment and change. It's the voice of many teachers who extend the boundaries of dominant practice, because they have a hunch that things could be better. Appreciating and practising that voice is a real support to you when you consider making improvements. Try it out loud, on your own, with a class: 'I think things can be better here, and I want us to try . . . '. Whether it's moving from doing to learning, or from individual to collaborative, it will help.

Tasks for social learning – and for learning about the social

If the tasks of a classroom are not specifically designed to include social dimensions, then the learners will be disadvantaged in learning about the social, and in the modal classroom this is too often the case so that the social aspects become a nuisance rather than a resource. The following chapter will examine the social structure and governance of the classroom, including rituals and routines, for promoting a pro-social environment. In this section we will address a very connected, but still somewhat separable aspect, the incorporation of social dimensions into the design of classroom tasks for learning. Classroom tasks which embrace social dimensions do so cumulatively as communicative, collaborative and community tasks.

Communicative tasks often include those which were described above as compositional and consequential. A core feature is the task of explaining one's understandings – at first to oneself and then to others. It leads to good peer dialogue and to higher-level thinking. Communication to other significant people can form the core of other consequential tasks, including those which treat the classroom as a community of enquirers to whom one's findings are communicated. As such practices develop they offer many chances of learning about the social dimensions of communication: learners can hear from others what was most successful about their planned part of the communication.

Collaborative tasks are ones where a single product is generated by more than one person. Again this may be handled cumulatively, starting with pair collaborations and moving to small groups. Here the learning about the social dimensions can be very rich, especially if learners are given some open prompts to review their experience. 'When did your collaboration work best: what helped it?' 'What might you improve if you did it again?'

Community tasks would involve the whole class as a community yet be composed of a range of contributions. The classic task in a knowledge-generating community is the task of the whole class communicating its improved knowledge on the topic to each other. Many other community tasks involve the community communicating to another audience – for example, another class or classes, an adult audience, and so on. Many such community tasks involve a performance of some sort, and this format can be extended beyond the traditional drama/music perfor-mance. One of the foremost developers of classrooms as communities of learners talks of the 'cycles of research–share–perform activities'[19] where the focus was mainly scientific enquiry. I have a long-lasting memory of seeing a class of 8-year-olds in Fox School give an assembly to the whole school (with parents squeezing in at the back) on what they had learned about their learning.

Tasks for meta-learning in a community

The distinction proposed in Chapters 3 and 4 between classrooms as a community of learners and classrooms as a learning community highlights the need for meta-learning to take a further step, to encom-pass learning about the community. Here again abstruse or mystifying concepts would be unhelpful, so what is needed is occasions to notice, discuss and reflect upon the class's own process of learning. The act of bringing them to public attention and of creating knowledge together about whatever has emerged is a hallmark of a learning community.

The tasks are communicative and collaborative, and do not take ages before they create meaningful development. An example is given by Sally who, after only a few lessons using community practices with her Geography class of Bedfordshire 14-year-olds, gave them a written enquiry which included the question: What could be the differences between 'working in a group' and 'being part of a learning community'? Some of the responses were:

> A group is random people put together, a community is people who trust each other, feel safe and are happy to work together and have the same aims.

> In a community we work with who we want, and in a group it is just sitting there.

> A group is just people working to create something, and a learning community is when everyone helps each other achieve.

The goals, purposes, processes and structures are being noticed and learned about. The teachers' learning community of which Sally was a part summarised these important points for their implications regarding learning as ' . . . *groups work together, communities learn together* . . . '.

Similarly, Kirsten with her History class of London 13-year-olds after eight lessons gave them a written enquiry including, 'Has learning in this class during this project been different from other learning experiences you have had?' Responses included:

> Yes, but in some ways no because we have done group work before, but I think maybe that this time it was different as we got to make it up as we went along.

> Yes, because we don't usually have so much of a say in what we are doing. I liked being able to make decisions about what we were doing.

> Yes, because usually when I am working on my own on something, I worry that I am not doing it well enough. This project meant that we worked together and made me more confident.

> Yes, because we found out a lot without being told very much.

The emergence, agency, empowerment and role changes are clear in these comments (more in Chapter 9). The teachers' learning community of which Kirsten was a part had used the same enquiry in their own collective, and had coined the term 'communal logging' (see p. 133) to describe it. So perhaps we could extend this to the other practices of meta-learning identified earlier, to give the collective parallels for those processes:

- communal noticing;
- communal discussion;
- communal logging;
- communal experimentation.

The task of assessment – demonstrating competence together

Recent decades have witnessed the term 'assessment' being hijacked in our schools. The original derivation of this term shows that assessment means *to sit next to* (Latin *assessere*, as shown in the French *asseyer*). So educational assessment is to sit next to someone to draw out their learning. But in our schools, when someone says 'assessment', most people think 'testing'. UK pupils are the most tested of all countries, and schools spend a massive £230 million a year on SATs and exams, rising rapidly.

At worst, emphasis on tests can lead people to feel pressurised and to adopt strategic responses to what they do in school. This was expressed by one American commentator in the title of his book *Learning to Succeed in School – Without Really Learning*.[20] But we want all our pupils to achieve well, so how can we avoid this worst-case scenario, without becoming an apologist for over-testing? The answer is that a focus on learning rather than a focus on performance is the dependable approach to enhancing performance.

Reclaiming the term 'assessment' from the domination of testing is sometimes attempted under the headline phrase 'Assessment for Learning', to indicate the classroom processes and tasks for focusing on learning and improving the classroom practice. This is very welcome but the term can sometimes slip back into assessment for performance. This happens through the dominant teacher-centred view of classrooms, and the accountability climate which focuses on test results as proving

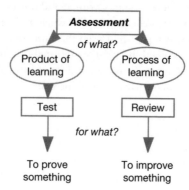

Figure 6.5 Two possible purposes for assessment

something about pupil learning. Here it can be useful to remember that when a learner shows a learning orientation they are focused on improving their competence, whereas when they adopt the less helpful performance orientation they focus on proving their competence. Figure 6.5 contrasts these two purposes.

However, there are in current times some differences in how the term 'assessment for learning' is being used. Much depends on the meaning given to that key term – learning. As earlier chapters explained, three main views of learning can be identified and each would lead to different processes of assessment.

Individualised forms of assessment typically lead to low levels of collaboration and community in classrooms, so that pupils do not develop skills of helping each other learn and achieve. Typically, these forms of assessment reduce the degree of interdependency among class members. Things could be different. One development has been to leave the assessment menu unchanged, and make individual scores a group responsibility. The combined impact of this and collaborative tasks can have a significant impact on learning. A study which compared individual against collaborative learning for only thirty minutes also informed the collaborative group that 50 per cent of each student's grade would be made up of how their group performed on the test.[21] The other 50 per cent would be individual. In this way, it was in the interests of every member of the group to ensure that all members make progress. After only thirty minutes a post-test was given which assessed

Table 6.1 Three views of learning and their different modes of assessment

View of learning	Testing in the form of:	Review in the form of:
1 Learning = being taught	Timed, written tasks, with 'right answers' which reflect the instruction given	Practice tests Mock exams
2 Learning = individual sense-making	Evidence of sense-making and meaning, as shown through dialogue	Individual reflection on the process of learning
3 Learning = building knowledge as part of doing things with others	Collaborative products such as a display of developing ideas and knowledge, a performance, story, publication or other form of account which shows the increased web of complexity	Group reflection on the processes of action, collaboration, and dialogue

both factual recall and critical thinking. The collaborative group were significantly better at critical thinking.

A second development is to add social and group tasks to the assess ment menu, and this is informed by the recognition that the other conceptions of learning indicate such practice (at the same time as indicating classroom approaches which get better results in tests!). Table 6.1 indicates the contrasts.

In a learning community it is important to develop assessment tasks which give voice to the improved knowledge which the community has at a point in time. Examples such as a class portfolio, 'Our Best Understandings',[22] can be considered. For meta-learning to be honoured in the task, the portfolio might also include excerpts from the communal log to indicate how the knowledge about their learning had extended. Bringing together the pieces which create the larger whole may be achieved by a range of methods: for a text, the metaphor I have used is that of a 'jigsaw publication' (which will make more sense following a reading of the next chapter). In such a text, the main parts are provided by sub-groups of a community who have worked together to create knowledge resources for the others on agreed themes. The form varies from text to video to web-pages, and creates the 'community product' for which every individual gladly signs a certificate stating, 'I hereby declare that the attached publication is a product of the learning community which has developed during this module, and that I have contributed to that product.'

Grace followed her reading of a text where a class develop a 'knowledge wall'[23] with an experiment with a science group of 10-year-olds. This led easily to the creation of a product which could have been used in assessment.

The class were encouraged to build their own knowledge wall (using Post-it™ notes) that contained comments, questions, researched information and then later to divide into groups in order to produce an answer to a question that interested them that could be shared with the class and used as part of jigsaw product that would draw together their findings.

The children attacked this with enthusiasm and greatly enjoyed their initial research and discussion. Despite having achieved level fours and fives on their recent SATs papers they initially found it difficult to devise experiments to test their questions but grew in confidence following guidance, in the form of suggestions from which they could choose, often disregarding my suggestions in favour of new plans. At the end of this experience they were all able to present their findings for study by other groups.

I asked the children whether they had enjoyed this mode of learning, and without exception they had, reporting a greater level of understanding and a belief that they would more easily remember the information and for longer.

A word about 'curriculum'

I suppose it may be expected in current times that classroom tasks is what curriculum is all about. But the pre-planned sequencing of subject-based tasks which has come to be seen as curriculum is as much part of the problem as part of today's solution. The points in these chapters apply to any 'subject'. Examples in these pages cover such diverse topics as learning about Plate tectonics, 1950s US civil rights, and Modern Greek. The issue about current curriculum is twofold: the

Table 6.2 Three views of learning and their different views of curriculum

View of learning	View of curriculum
1 Learning =being taught	Curriculum as fact
2 Learning = individual sense-making	Curriculum as activity
3 Learning = building knowledge as part of doing things with others	Curriculum as inquiry

view of learning and the view of the learner. On the first of these, different paradigms of curriculum have been identified.[24]

On the second issue, the view of learner that curriculum implies, Mary Jalongo writes:

I am reminded of a battered curriculum chart that was posted on the inside of my classroom door during my early years of teaching. It was the well-organized product of several adult minds at the Department for Education. The neat squares delineated what content should be taught at each grade level. Before I started to teach, the chart seemed rather reassuring. I knew, for example, that I had to teach cursive writing, a unit on solid and liquid measurement, a social studies unit on 'families around the world'. But then the children arrived. The majority of them were desperately poor. Estrella, using her very best handwriting, wrote and illustrated a story about how her teeth 'rawted out'; they were blackened stumps so badly abscessed that she could barely talk or keep food down. During the unit on measurement, we made no-bake cookies, and Hector confided that he did not have 'cooked stuff because the stove was broke'; to add credence to this claim, his mother sent me a note the next day asking for the recipe, then sent me an effusive thank-you note which implied that they had been without a stove for quite some time. A shy little redhead named Eddie, who was a long-term substitute teacher's son, was one of the few who did not qualify for free lunches; when his single-parent mother went on a job interview to a neighbouring state, she was killed in a car crash. I decided to skip my happy textbook unit on the nuclear family. The nurse and I found a dentist for Estrella. Another teacher donated a stove to Hector's family. When I arrived at school each day, Eddie was standing outside, waiting for the doors to open, and his grand-mother and I agreed to let him come early and stay late; we needed that time together. I tore the chart down.[25]

Alfie Kohn makes the link between this state of affairs and the view of learning it embodied in his own albeit popular teaching: 'The syllabus was designed before I met the kids – which is a sure sign that something is wrong. I was treating them like interchangeable open bird beaks'.[26]

It is possible to make more of a shift towards learning in planning curriculum. A current example of this is the RSA 'Opening Minds' curriculum which is being successfully developed in UK primary and secondary schools. It advances 'a new curriculum divided into five broad categories: competences for

- learning,
- citizenship,
- relating to people,
- managing situations,
- managing information.'[27]

And in other schools a clear approach to learning as sense-making and community building is advanced through the International Baccalaureate Primary Years Programme, which comprises 'a "trans-disciplinary approach to constructing knowledge" with Six Units of Inquiry:

- Who we are
- Where we are in place and time
- How we express ourselves
- How the world works
- How we organise ourselves
- Sharing the planet.'[28]

Prompts for reflection

What ideas can you develop for how the tasks in your classroom can become more:

- *compositional* – creating something whose details emerge as it develops;
- *consequential* – relating to learners' feeling that they can do something different as a result;
- *reflective* – pausing to stop and notice the process;
- *communicative* – including explaining to oneself and to others;
- *collaborative* – creating a single product from multiple efforts;
- *community* – engaging the whole-class contributions, including the community reflections.

Your ideas for developing these tasks can be more likely to happen if you talk them over with a colleague. Who will you choose?

7 Social structure in a learning community

One of the most revealing things about a learning community is the various ways in which participants come to relate to each other. Various structures for this are crucial to the classroom, and this chapter builds from small beginnings to the whole class.

The social structure of the classroom is, at one and the same time, both a major achievement and a major missed opportunity. After all, the classroom is measurably the most complex social situation on the face of the planet, and the way in which it is structured is what makes the major contribution to its effects.[1] I find that teachers generally recognise this complexity and, when asked what they want life in their classrooms to be like, often describe the elements of community: productive interaction and relationships, peer helping, embracing diversity, and so on. But they also are prepared to say that they do not always achieve this vision of the classroom environment, and then go on to talk about the pressures on them which influence their choice of practices.

The dominant method of running a classroom uses a gross simplification of what we know about learning, and this shows up clearly in the forms of social structure that you see in most classrooms today. It is 'one-to-many' – in which a single person, the teacher, is positioned in contrast to the many people, the pupils. It is not the numbers on their own which create the scenario, but a set of beliefs about the various participants, their roles and capacities. The teacher 'has' the knowledge whereas the pupils do not, the teacher is assumed to have control whereas the pupils are assumed not to be capable, the teacher's job is to 'deliver' and the pupils must 'receive' – all the features of that view of learning 'Learning = being taught'. This form of social structure is the same as it has been since the earliest known classrooms of 3000 BC, increasingly widespread during industrialisation and subsequently exported all over the globe. And while we are considering the big picture, it may be the case that this form of social structure is exactly inappropriate for post-industrial societies. You have only to examine the learning relationships in non-school settings to recognise that the social structure of the dominant classroom is increasingly limited. In this sense classrooms seem locked in to a past set of assumptions.

Creating interdependence

To operate a classroom as a learning community, something else needs to be achieved, and the social structure of the classroom makes a major contribution to achieving a different vision. The key achievement that the social structure needs to create is interdependence. As with all aspects of a learning community, the rationale here is both social and intellectual.

- Interdependence fosters respect for others and their contribution.
- Interdependence is required for handling individual contributions to a communal effort.
- Interdependence is a feature of building collective knowledge.

These ideas are not as unusual as may first appear (although they are not represented well in the discourse about classrooms). Just consider some everyday phrases of interdependence, such as:

- All for one and one for all.
- The whole is greater than the sum of the parts.
- We need to hang together or we'll be hung separately.

Phrases such as these conjure up the image of the technical definition in the dictionary: 'Interdependent: relying on mutual assistance, support, cooperation, or interaction among constituent elements or members', and which is the vision behind many of the occasions when teachers emphasise team working and learning the skills of working together and learning together.

A further aspect of interdependence may need additional support; this is the idea that knowledge is built and exists in relationships. It is a key understanding about learning and knowledge, that it is constructed with others, distributed with others, and socially controlled. But it contrasts markedly with the dominant idea in our culture that knowledge is individual possession residing in individual heads. Marlene Scardamalia emphasises that in these conditions not only is knowledge shared but responsibility is also shared:

> Collective responsibility refers to the condition in which respon-
> sibility for the success of a group effort is distributed across all
> the members rather than being concentrated in the leader. . . .
> Collective *cognitive* responsibility involves an added dimension:
> members also take responsibility for knowing what needs to be
> known and for insuring that others know what needs to be known.[2]

But after some time and supportive experience in a classroom, these concepts may be heard in the voice of pupils, as is the case with these 11-year-olds, about the social process of knowledge building:

> 'Good science making is all about working with ideas, testing them
> out in different conditions, retesting, talking with people who are
> working on similar ideas, and bringing ideas to the whole group.'[3]

And about the social purpose:

> 'Even if you learn something perfectly, or are a pioneer in your
> area, all your work is useless if nobody else can understand you. You
> might as well have done no work at all. The point of learning is to
> share it with others. Lone learning is not enough.'[4]

The vision here contrasts greatly with practices for the social structure of classrooms today. One significant example is the use of 'seating plans', often in the secondary classroom. 'We use boy-girl-boy-girl', says one teacher. 'We use alphabetical order', says another. And they fail to see that such plans treat pupils as objects. Spirited defences of such arrange-ments are offered, but they usually give the game away – control. And control of a particularly ineffective sort, which relies on hierarchical position of the teacher and the anonymous position of the pupils. In discussions of seating plans it can also happen that the reason such practices are adopted by teachers is that they either do not know of or are not confident about alternatives. 'You're not saying they can sit with who they like are you?', comes the distrustful retort adopting an opposite extreme. No. The alternative is that pupils in a learning community come to relate to and learn with all others in the class. In the process pupils come to be known more by their peers, and develop more engaged and productive identities:

> individuals learn in the interest of participation in communities that matter to them. They learn in order to know how to be productive in the community, and to gain access to valued forms of community participation. Their reward is in seeing their contribution, knowing that others recognise their contribution, and, through this process, forging a new sense of themselves.

As adults we create our identities and connections around our work, knowledge and contributions to communities. There is no good reason why schools should not offer the same for pupils.

The purpose of this chapter is to outline some of the classroom practices which help create the social structure of classrooms as learning communities. These practices will be most effective when combined with those discussed in other chapters on goals, tasks, resources and roles. But they deserve a distinct consideration.

Pairs and groups

A fundamental building block of learning relations in classrooms is talk for learning in pairs. Teachers who use such classroom practices regularly use a range of different terms to refer to them: chatterboxes/ buzz time/learning partners. All of these are brief and focused moments for exchange in pairs. Such a practice carries many important messages of itself – that pupil voices are important and deserve time and space in the life of the classroom, that talk is an important vehicle, and so on. As such, these practices are regularly evaluated in a positive way.

The dominant beliefs in classrooms, however, can de-emphasise these messages, to the point that when teachers try out such practices they are initially surprised that it 'works'! For example, Eleanor says to her reception class, 'Tell each other for three minutes what you most enjoyed about the weekend'. Without hesitation, twenty little learners turn to each other and engage in conversation. Rebecca asks her year 1 class to tell each other in pairs what they have noticed about their learning this morning. Off they go. Sonia is introducing a theme about 'taking notes', and first asks her year 3 class to tell each other in pairs any examples they know of people who take notes, and what value do they find. Immediate buzz.

But whether it's 4-year-olds or adults, there is no reason to assume that talking together will necessarily lead to learning in some direct manner. Here's where both guidance and review can play a very important part. The difference between guidance and review as a source for improvement can be important: the first is more teacher-oriented and the second more learner-oriented: 'I have found out that the best way to give advice to your children is to find out what they want and then advise them to do it'.[5]

In the spirit of learning communities wishing to create a less hierarchical learning culture, I'll start with an example of review (especially as the results often surprise teachers as to the sophistication of even quite young learners). Yvonne teaches in a north London school and has been operating talk partners with her year 1 pupils for a few weeks. She asks them about the practice and what they notice.[6] Their comments are very illuminating:

> '*In Talk Partners your partner can help you because they tell you different ways to work things out*'. This comment highlights a potentially very complex process – the exchange of strategies for tackling a task, involving high-level communication and understanding. Yet this young person seems to communicate the point as though it were simple and straightforward.

> '*I didn't have a clue how to do it at first, but then my partner helped me. After he had told me about his work I knew what sort of things to say about mine*'. Here we see illumination of the process of developing narrative together. The ways of knowing in pairs are built between them – a process which is the microcosm of how knowing is built anywhere.

'*When my partner tells me how to do something in a better way, I know they are not being mean, they are just trying to help me*'. This speaks of a crucial process in the development of pairs and, later, communities, the growth of trust. The nature of judgement which can be debilitating in the public gaze of the classroom can be handled much more productively between peers.

'*Talk Partners are good because then I can remember the work better. When we have to do it again I will remember it better and I won't have to ask the teacher*'. Although this young person uses the vocabulary of 'work' the point made is a key one about memory, that it is supported through talk which helps to consolidate an idea. This comment also speaks of the crucial process in changing the social structure of the classroom – less dependency on the teacher, and by implication greater empowerment for pupils.

Composing and recomposing pairs

Occasionally a teacher will demonstrate some reluctance to developing pair work in their classroom, putting this in the voice of the child who says, 'I don't want to work with X'. On such occasions the question of choice of pairings is elevated into a much larger issue than it turns out to be in productive classrooms. When pairs are regularly used in a whole group situation (for example, in the primary practice of the whole class 'on the mat') the composition of those pairs is going to be changing, just because pupils enter that space in different orders. Occasional prompts to 'talk with someone you haven't lately' also distribute the connections, to the point that it may not become necessary for the teacher to direct any recomposing of pairs. Regular and changing use of pairs is a basic building block in the message that we are all here to relate to each other, to help each other and to learn with each other.

As we shall see later, a similar point applies to the composition and recomposition of groups. On those occasions teachers may also have to cope with an additional voice on such practices, in this case the policy voice which suggests (contrary to the research evidence[7]) that 'ability' is an important criterion for composing pairs and groups. Research has demonstrated that in pair discussions, children deemed 'low ability' can be effective in helping those deemed 'high ability'.

Similarly, classrooms which regularly change the composition of groups, sometimes with particular purposes in mind for a particular grouping, seem to generate an overall community atmosphere of pupil willingness to engage widely throughout the structure. The important message for this chapter is:

Classrooms as communities develop widespread inter-dependence partly by ensuring that they do not operate fixed social structures.

Collaboration and dialogue for learning

One of the challenges which emerges, is that of conveying the message that the purpose of talk in pairs and groups is to promote learning. The above examples from Yvonne's class seem to display little difficulty with the idea, but there may have been other examples (or even earlier examples from these children) along the lines of 'We haven't done any work in that bit – we've got nothing in our books'. This, of course, is the voice of the dominant view of school learning: (a) that it's work and (b) that it has to be validated by writing. In response to this and similar voices we find ourselves sometimes needing to explain and support the ways through which talk does promote learning.

The first point to make is that not all talk leads to learning. Although it is difficult to categorise in such a way that divides talk which promotes learning from that which does not, there are reasonable indications. As Neil Mercer puts it:

> observational research in classrooms suggests that when pupils are allowed to work together in groups most of their talk is either disputational or blandly and unreflectively co-operative, only involving some of the children and providing no more than a brief and superficial consideration of the relevant topics.[8]

In the face of such a picture we need to examine various approaches to talk and help pupils learn about it too. This will change the situation which Mercer describes as follows: 'In all levels of education, from primary school to university, students usually seem to be expected to work out the "ground rules" of effective discussion for themselves'.

A contribution, depending on the language level of the learners involved, might be to examine some of the different terms for talking together, for example, as mentioned in Chapter 3, 'discussion', 'debate' and 'dialogue'.

- *Discussion* is generally held to be a spoken consideration in a group, but its Latin roots carry a meaning of disputation or agitation, as are evident in the medical use of this word, meaning the act or process of breaking up, or dispersing, a tumour, or the like. Also consider other words from this root: percussion and concussion!
- *Debate* is a form of discourse in which two opposing teams defend and attack a given proposition often in a formalised manner, or make opposing points. Its conflictual nature is reflected in its root the Old French *débatre*, to beat. See also batter!
- *Dialogue* describes an exchange of ideas or opinions. The roots of this word are the Greek *dialogos* (*dia* = through, *logos* = speech, word, reason). Compare epilogue, prologue etc.

With these broad distinctions in place, it becomes more possible to focus our attention on a more detailed examination of talk in classrooms. Although an exhaustive categorisation of talk would probably not be meaningful, the following may be recognisable:

Phatic talk: spoken in order to share feelings, create goodwill, or set a pleasant social mood, rather than to convey information/meaning:

'How have you been this week?' 'Not so bad. And you?'.

Expressive talk: individual judgements and statements of feeling, without explanation:

'This is boring' or 'This is great', 'I can't stand maths' 'No, nor can I'.

Accusatory talk: statements about others' actions, often with an attribution about intention:

'You did that wrong' 'You didn't read the instructions'.

Disputational talk (debate): short exchanges of assertions and counter-assertions with little pooling of meaning or explaining:

'No, that's not it' 'Yes it is'.

Cumulative talk: agreements and sometimes elaborations which build uncritically on what the other has said:

'And then we could add' 'Yes, and then . . . '.

Structures for improving talk

Alongside the development of the dialogue which learning communities depend on, it is sometimes necessary to help learners out of the less helpful types listed above. Sally, a teacher in a Bedfordshire secondary school, found that her pupils were quite practised in accusatory talk between them, and did not quite know how to avoid the hazards it brings. As part of improving their peer work she helped them move beyond as follows:

> I explained that when communicating feelings, it is important to keep in mind not only how those feelings are delivered, but how they are received as well. There are two approaches when communicating a message to another: a 'you message' and an 'I message'. A 'you message' is often accusatory, as in 'you made me angry' and can put someone in a defensive posture. An 'I message' does not blame or judge, but rather expresses a specific feeling and reason for that feeling, as in 'I feel angry when you tease me because I don't like to be teased by my friends'. I already had the following phrase typed out and pinned up in the classroom:
>
> 'I feel . . . . when you . . . . because . . . . '.[9]

This example strikes me as not only empowering to the learners in Sally's class, but is also achieved through a usefully open form of guidance.

Now we can also build in some open guidance on the sort of talk likely to generate dialogue, shared understanding and community knowledge.

Structuring dialogic talk[10]

The sort of talk, in pairs or in groups, which is most associated with rich learning, development of understanding and building community knowledge is dialogue. Although it is not sensible to believe that dialogue can be reduced to component parts, or indeed engineered into life, some attention and guidance on the elements below might be useful for learners of any age who have not become practised in its forms.

Elements in dialogic talk

Focus on meaning
Reasoning is explicit: 'I think this because . . . '.
Others are invited to examine one's reasoning: 'What do you think of my idea?'
Enquire into other's reasoning: 'Can I ask you how you got there?'
The perspective of others is voiced: 'So you feel that the idea . . . '.

Moderate conflict
Tentative language is used: 'It might be that . . . ' 'It seems that . . . '.
Assertions are seen as hypotheses-to-be-tested: 'It's only an idea but . . . '.
Similarities as well as differences are acknowledged.
Disagreements are framed in terms of ideas not persons.
Multiple stances are assumed 'From this point of view it might follow that . . . '.

Move forward together
Further enquiries are proposed: 'We could examine that . . . '.
Changes of position are mentioned: 'I see it differently now'.
Mutual goals are emphasised: 'I think we can crack this'.
Enhancement of communal knowledge is sought: 'We need to understand this'.

The link with learning is twofold, in that the act of talking in this fashion with others has a twofold effect: explaining one's ideas to others helps to create and refine them, while authentic interchange between people generates new understandings and possibilities. Vygotsky is often cited as having discussed this, and the way that ideas may emerge first on the extra-mental plane, before being reviewed and accommodated on the intra-mental plane. But I find that Annie (10-years-old) says it very clearly:

> You learn more [when working with others] because if you explain to people what to do you say things that you wouldn't say to yourself, really. So you learn things that you wouldn't know if you were just doing it by yourself.

Dialogic talk in classrooms frequently develops under the following conditions:[11]

- students express their own thoughts and questions rather than recite textbook ideas;
- the teacher–student exchanges help students better articulate their understandings;
- student–student exchanges involve them trying to understand each other's thinking.

Peers teaching peers

A practice which came to be known as 'Reciprocal Teaching' emerged in the context of helping learners read and comprehend.[12] It was based on an analysis of research into what expert readers do, and the identification of the following four strategies that, when used in concert, would tap all the functions needed for comprehension:

- questioning;
- clarifying;
- summarising;
- predicting.

In the original small-scale version of this practice, students would be invited to read a text paragraph by paragraph, and during the reading to practise the four strategies: generating questions, summarising, attempting to clarify word meanings or confusing text, and predicting what might appear in the next paragraph. Considerable advances in student comprehension followed.[13]

The practice has proved important at larger levels. Reciprocal Teaching became a key ingredient in classrooms fostering a community of learners.[14] In such classrooms it was a case of students taking turns in leading small-group discussions on provided texts.

All four activities may be handled in a pair or small group, and I find them supported by general prompts such as those below.

Structure of prompts for reciprocal teaching

Question
(before reading)
What do I think about the topic of this text already?
What do I want to know more about?
(as I read)
How would I explain that?
What's an example of that?

Clarify
(after reading)
What did you each take these authors to mean?
What did you do with hard-to-understand parts?

Summarise
What are the main messages?
What are the key ideas?

Predict
What might happen if these ideas were taken forward?
What could you do in using them?

Many variations of this practice and its associated prompts can be created, as long as the key principles are maintained. In that sense this is a flexible practice applicable to any learning context where texts are used – this should cover most 'subjects'! Our conception of texts need not be limited to written texts: the practice has been extended to promote the learning from graphical sources too.[15]

This practice embodies key messages about learning and the role of learners, especially about the importance of: meaning, active individuals, exchange and of constructed knowledge. Since these are not the dominant messages in classrooms, it may take a little time for learners to adjust their expectations, but they do so as they experience the increased engagement and understanding. As the review in Chapter 4 showed, considerable benefits follow.

A further step is possible, and indeed necessary, to move from reciprocal teaching as a contribution to a community of learners to an element in a learning community. In a community of learners, members of a class could be more engaged and more effective in the particulars of the class through the use of reciprocal teaching, but they would not necessarily become more reflective or more able to apply their learning to other contexts. This is where meta-learning is needed, and can be developed through simple but important processes such as review. For example, a review of experiences using reciprocal teaching which uses prompts such as 'How does it work best?', 'How could it be helped to work better?' would bring to the surface the very processes of dialogic learning for which it is designed, and would help learners take these processes to other situations by the fact that they are developing their language and understanding. Naheeda asked her class of 10-year-olds, 'How has reciprocal teaching helped your learning?'. The children answered:

> 'It gives you confidence to ask the teacher questions.'
>> 'It has helped me to understand books better.'
>> 'It is better when a child asks you instead of the teacher.'
>> 'I feel like I can be a teacher as well; it makes me think about the book and ask questions.'
>> 'It gives me confidence to ask other children questions and gives me independence.'
>> 'It gives you confidence. It gives you independence because you ask the questions.'

With this addition and with increasing experience, reciprocal teaching turns out to be an important building block in developing the hallmarks of a learning community: agency, collaboration, dialogue, enquiry and reflection. With this base, the ideas can be scaled up to the whole classroom.

Jigsaw classroom

The metaphor of the jigsaw refers to making up whole pictures from parts. Applied to the classroom, a technique originated in 1970s USA after-school desegregation, as an intervention to improve inter-ethnic relations in classrooms.[16] Its design was exactly on the theme of this chapter: how to structure the classroom to increase interdependence. Effects on inter-ethnic relations in classes were positive, and it was soon shown to have an impact on classroom performance.

The core idea is to divide an area of enquiry into different sections, each one of which is allocated to a sub-group of the class.[17] These sub-groups become expert in their section, and then the groups are recomposed with one expert from each section in the (now) 'jigsaw' group. At this point the big picture is created – by students who have now a grasp of that picture which was created by their own efforts and meaning systems.

Examples of the jigsaw methodology come from all sectors of education. Here is Andrew, a teacher in a west London secondary school, outlining the considerations in his use.

My original use of jigsaw methodology came out of the impossibility I often felt of 'covering the content' of KS3 National Curriculum or GCSE/A-level syllabus in the allotted time. Now it is my methodology of choice, as in recent years my sense of that pressure has reduced, while 'content coverage' has increased. Large topics can be addressed in a much shorter time than if the teacher spends time on each component part.

To help build a learning community through the use of jigsawing, a topic is required that has a number of component parts that can be understood in isolation without necessarily understanding the whole topic. In History teaching, topics that are best understood chronologically for example would not be appropriate, but a good example would be causation. A big question under consideration could be '*What caused World War II?*'. Possible answers include German anger at the Treaty of Versailles, Chamberlain's policy of appeasement, the failure of the League of Nations, the Nazi–Soviet Pact of August 1939, the rise of dictators such as Hitler and Mussolini in the 1930s, and the Great Depression.

I divide the class into the number of component parts of the topic that I would like the pupils to address. In this example there are six. Each group would research their particular 'cause' and produce information for the rest of the class – they become the 'experts' in the particular aspect they are investigating, and also decide how they will convey their knowledge to the others: a handout, PowerPoint, role-play, and so on.

The important aspect of 'jigsawing' is that the pupils become expert in the whole jigsaw (topic) and not just expert in their particular piece (cause), but the process ensures that each individual's contribution is crucial to the community understanding. When new groups are formed, containing one member of each 'cause' group, each one communicates what they understand about their cause. At the end, a whole-class discussion may be used, or perhaps a joint presentation: for other topics I have used creation of verses for a class song or scenes for a class play.

A summative assessment task must be set which consolidates and confirms the students' understanding of the whole topic. In this example, the big question becomes an essay question and each cause might become a paragraph theme. Students are asked to demonstrate their understanding of the possible causes and to create their own argument, perhaps ranking their paragraphs (causes) in order of importance. Obviously at this time, students choose their own main cause, rather than the one that was 'allocated' to them in the preparatory work.

For me, this technique has a number of very positive attributes. The focus shifts from the teacher to the student. The teacher very much facilitates the learning at all stages, from the organisation of the task to the checking for understanding, but the focus is very much on the students. The element of 'collective responsibility' helps students to produce quality contributions. All student work is judged not only by the teacher but more importantly by their peers. A poor contribution can ultimately let the whole class

down. I say as the tasks are set 'the class is relying on you . . . '.
Further, the nature of sharing of the pieces of the jigsaw means
that student participation within class and interaction with each
other increases dramatically. And again when time is short for
revision, jigsawing is an excellent way to constructively address
large topics.

The methodology requires participation by all members:
together with the building of student confidence in putting
forward ideas and respecting others' ideas, it is crucial in developing a learning community.

One of the remarkable things about Andrew's account is that it is his
response to the pressures of current times: while many teachers respond
to this pressure in terms of themselves 'covering the content' and thus
adopting more teacher-centred approaches, Andrew knows that the key
challenge is for his students to 'cover' and understand and communicate
the ideas in the field.

The phases are clear in Andrew's account:

1   Divide theme into a number of areas.
2   Allocate these areas to small groups who 'specialise' in them for a
    time.
3   Create small jigsaw groups from each of the specialist groups, to
    create a whole picture.
4   Have the whole class benefit from the small jigsaw groups.

There are numerous variations that can be developed using these
basis principles. Specialist groups could be formed around pupil
questions rather than teacher allocations; the amount of time taken for
each step could vary considerably (I have sometimes used the methodology in a single session, whereas there are many school examples which
carry on for weeks); and so on. The practice of jigsaw has been applied
to many different school subjects and to many ages of learners: its limits
are probably only the limits of our imagination.

Jigsaw methodology was created to improve relations between
groups, and that can be the case for groups that have been created on

any dimension: 'race', language, 'ability'. With regard to language, jigsaw has been used in multilingual classrooms: cooperative groups are formed from one English speaker, one non-English speaker and one bilingual student.[18] In a school world where notions of 'ability' circulate, and policy voices recommend without evidence practices of 'ability grouping'; teachers considering jigsaw methodology can be concerned about the composition of groups on these grounds. But if the messages of competition and difference in a class are being replaced by messages of helping and collaboration, and the tasks really do engage a wide range of student contribution, then the mediation which goes on in the 'expert' groups can be beneficial for all its individuals – because the forthcoming task of communicating to colleagues in the jigsaw group is a task which everyone in the 'expert' group shares. Therefore they are not competing experts, but experts in their co-created topic. Ann, a headteacher from north London, after fourteen lessons of learning-centred collaboration with a class of 9-year-olds, wrote:

My observation of the collaborative learning in the seven weeks confirmed most of what I had gleaned from the literature. My pupils were less competitive as they provided mutual help to one another. The boundaries between the 'most' and 'least' able became less marked. . . . For the first time, I felt that I had overcome the problem of the narrow focus that only reaches the middle group. I did not have to rely on my 'differentiated' plans and worksheets as the children had driven their own learning and progress and attained more. My previous 'differentiated work' designed to reach all the pupils only served to *reach* but never *stretched* all. . . . The important shift lay in the fact that the children were taking responsibility.

Another reflection on the dynamic between learners comes from Alyson, a teacher in a Surrey comprehensive school, who conducted two of her 'mixed ability' science classes with 12-year-olds using the jigsaw methodology. Over seven sessions, which addressed her least-liked topic, the classes were highly engaged. She wrote:

Anyone who is used to a traditional classroom, whereby students are always sat still, in rows of desks listening attentively to the teacher, may have viewed my classroom during those learning sessions as unruly, noisy, disorganised etc. As a teacher I may have been perceived as uninterested or lacking control. To the more discerning eye, to one who knew those children as well as I did, I hope they would have noticed the agency that students were taking for their learning, the way in which they were helping and encouraging each other, the choices they were making for themselves, and the pleasure they took from constructing their knowledge together in order to make sense of what they needed to learn.

The literature on jigsaw methodology includes a seemingly never-ending number of variations – Jigsaw II,[19] Jigsaw III,[20] Jigsaw IV.[21] Putting aside the apparent need (especially in the USA) to package such variations, their directions sometimes strike me as reflecting the culture of schooling rather than the purposes of this methodology. Some have introduced competition between groups, to be decided by 'Team' results on an individual test. Others introduce more 'tests' to 'check' that the students 'have' the appropriate knowledge at each stage. This speaks of a different conception of learning. Yet others introduce more guidance to pupils, on how their groups should work and what skills they should use. This reflects the tension to be found in most of the approaches to collaborative groupwork: should the teacher structure and pre-specify the skills, tasks and processes, or should they be left to emerge and learned about where necessary. My personal preference tends towards the latter, for two reasons. First, if we are really moving towards more learner-centred and learning-centred classrooms then the handing over of teacher specification is important. Second, in line with that old idea that 'teachable moments' are the most valuable resource for a teacher, the specification in advance may be less effective, and indeed may be based on shaky predictions of what 'guidance' a group will need.

Nevertheless, some anticipation is of value. As with all practices which are not the dominant sort, pupils may show surprise and a little discomfort at first. As Ellen put it about her 12-year-olds:

They were not used to the structure, and they were not used to having to think on their own. They were afraid of being wrong. However, with my facilitation as well as seeing that I was not looking for right or wrong answers, just well-supported ones, my students began to enjoy the activity.

This example reminds us of an issue in adopting any new practice: initial comments which demonstrate that this is beyond the current comfort zone should not be taken as reasons for not persevering. Indeed, it is an opening for supporting the vision and method of the classroom as a learning community. For example, in the jigsaw methodology at the stage when pupils move from specialist groups to jigsaw groups, there may be value in a statement and some open prompts which help participants adopt the stance required in this new part of the structure:

We're going to get into jigsaw groups now, where the idea is to build a big picture from the pieces you bring from each of your specialist groups. You'll want to show them what you have produced, but make sure you tell them the story of how you did it too:

- Any new ideas or understandings you've come up with.
- How those relate to the ideas from other groups.
- What understandings can you all put together now?
- What can you now do with these ideas and understandings?
- What would be a good demonstration of your new knowledge?

There may too be new experience to get used to for teachers who use jigsaw – such as the 'over-engagement' of pupils. These issues lead us into the next section, while the role aspects will be addressed further in Chapter 9.

Cross-talk

When small-group structures are used in the service of building a classroom learning community, there are a number of pitfalls which can be anticipated and avoided. These come in two main types: those which constrain the construction of communal knowledge, and those which limit the reflective learning. Both may be addressed by the structural practice in this section.

Sometimes sub-groups in a class generate more of an affiliation to each other than is advantageous for the whole class learning about the theme in hand. On these occasions they may display some of the qualities of cliques: impermeable boundaries, unshared meanings and elements of competition with other sub-groups. Sometimes this is a temporary phase to go through: having helped learners move away from the individual stance they are used to, the achievement of sub-group goals and purposes is a good step, but some of their socialisation into competition may remain. Here again the structuring of between-group interaction (and of the task) is important.

Sometimes sub-groups become so engaged in their task that they act as though sharing it with others is an interruption and a nuisance. So their engagement in creating a product from which their peers are meant to benefit becomes almost counter-productive to that goal. This occurs most when the balance of sub-group focus shifts more towards the product than the process of learning. Here the form of the between-group interaction needs to stimulate something better. Even in the jigsaw methodology, when specialist groups bring their contribution to the learning jigsaw they may do so in the dominant but ineffective ways of 'telling' about the product – giving a presentation, 'reporting back' and so on – instead of giving a richer account of their learning in both its product and its process.

Ann Brown and Joseph Campione coined the term 'cross-talk' in their classrooms fostering a community of learners. It signified the practice of getting between-group interaction to happen. In the context, culture and goals for their work, it is described as 'students from the various research groups periodically report in about their progress to date, and students from other working groups ask questions of clarification or extension'.[22] The principles in this practice can be carried through to a range of classrooms other than those focusing on science learning, and using the terminology of research and findings.

But in my experience a difficulty can arise in the practice of cross-talk. If it is left to the dominant norms of classroom learning, pupils will report findings and answers with an associated sense of possession and sometimes competition. They will not – without support at first, that is – report on their process or on anything else about their learning. Since this for me makes a crucial difference between a community of learners and a learning community, I think it essential to offer prompts for cross-talk which aim to achieve this:

We're going to do cross-talk, where the idea is to keep in touch with and learn from each others' learning in the different groups. Think of what has been happening in your group and anything that comes to mind about:

- Any new ideas or understandings you've come up with.
- Anything that has helped you progress towards achieving your purpose.
- What difficulties you have met.
- Anything about how your group has worked together.
- How it is feeling now.

Whole-talk

As this chapter has progressed, I hope I have communicated a sense of the cumulative structuring which could go on in a classroom operating as a learning community. At each stage – pairs, specialist groups, jigsaw groups, occasions for cross-talk – I hope that its contribution to creating interdependence in the classroom has been clear, and that you might be able to help learners make the most of these structures. Each of them is a different 'participant structure', each with its own guidance, and as these become routine, pupils will recognise them, understand the role expected of them, and start to experience the benefits they bring.

But this considerable achievement may not quite achieve one last thing in a classroom operating as a learning community – the sense of community which is building for all. In the busy, engaged sequence of experiences the sense of the whole may just never be voiced. It may be that a structure and a task to elicit this could be valuable.

The structure that is appropriate here is of course the whole-class group. Many classroom teachers have some experience of this if they have utilised 'circle time' with their class. But although the idea of sitting in a circle may be valued, the issue is what sort of talk or other communication do we seek? Here is where the very structure of a large circle can prove most difficult for the sort of talk we want, as many people continue to find such settings intimidating and the patterns of contribution become more polarised, with a small number of participants 'taking the floor'. Another vehicle for hearing the voice of all is required.

I had a very important unforeseen experience on this theme in one of our MA modules 'Building Learning Communities'. The process of this module is to learn about its theme by doing it and reflecting on it, and during one phase a specialist sub-group had formed to consider teachers' understandings of classrooms as learning communities. One of their actions was to circulate a quick enquiry of a few questions to the whole group, and to collate the responses. The picture created was very illuminating of how and why the participants felt they were part of a community. The key learning followed for me – to have these responses communicated back to all participants immediately. It offered a source of learning for all participants which could not have been achieved any other way, and the circle conversation which followed reflected this. It gave us the idea 'communal logging'.

So there may be a need for someone in the community to find quick and easy ways of collecting participants' voices and making them available for all. I'm sure various forms are possible: for some of the classrooms I have been in, the practice of each participant writing on a Post-it™ note to construct a class poster would be very workable.

Learning about the social structures

Learning communities bring together the social and the intellectual, and in so doing engage more of the social dimension more productively than the modal classroom. As mentioned in the previous chapter, there needs to be some learning about the social dimension of learning life. Many elements of this chapter provide opportunities for learning about the social processes which are promoted through these structures of participation, using an appropriate focus for review. For example, Using talk partners for learning – how does it work best? Reciprocal teaching – how do we build on others' ideas? Jigsaw classroom – how did our groups work and how might we improve them? Cross-talk – how do we best learn from each other? And so on.

As will be developed further in Chapter 9, the teacher's role can often be a roving facilitator who adds prompts and reflections to the processes occurring in the class. But there can also be occasions when a more planned focus on a theme becomes necessary, especially those which an individual participant might be unlikely to raise in a review:

- Roles that emerge in groups – reviewing and perhaps redistributing them.
- Conflicts – what creates them and what reduces them.
- Beginnings and endings – how best to handle them.
- Stages in group development.
- Making sense of difficulties in participation, including group member absence.

Balancing acts

For anyone such as a teacher facilitating a classroom as learning community, there are plenty of balancing acts to enjoy! In the theme of this chapter, which is central to the structuring of a collective, these may include

Shall we start at all?	$\leftrightarrow$	Shall we start gradually?
Can I trust them?	$\leftrightarrow$	Can we build trust?
Shall I instruct first?	$\leftrightarrow$	Will they learn from review?
How much action?	$\leftrightarrow$	How much reflection?
How much time on parts?	$\leftrightarrow$	How much time on wholes?

I have an answer to these questions from my own experience in this role: it is to try something and then review whether the balance is turning out to be appropriate for the particular occasion. My experience is that the balance is nearly always more to the right-hand side of the above dimensions than I had expected.

Prompts for reflection

- This chapter has built up many practices for creating inter-dependence in the classroom: pairs, reciprocal teaching, jigsaw groups, communal reviews and communal logging.
- Which of these have you met before, and perhaps used before? How do you make sense of the impact that they have?
- Which of them are you currently using in your classroom? Do you wish to use those more or extend your range into practices which are new for you?
- What will help you to adjust your current 'balancing acts' so that you are in a better position to try out some developments in the social structure?

8 Resources in a learning community

Goals, tasks and social structures are key dimensions of a learning community classroom, but what else is required to make it operate? The term 'resources' has sometimes been used in a narrow sense to mean only texts to be used by learners (as in 'resource-based learning') but here I wish to use it in a wider sense to refer to all human and physical resources – texts, objects, communications channels, ICT, and so on – which the learning community might call on.

'Inside' any classroom which operates as a learning community, the human resources are obviously crucial, and the last two chapters have attempted to outline ways in which learning tasks and social structure can make the most of this in the face-to-face meetings. Whether those human resources *feel* they are a resource to each other is a matter worthy of further consideration. But there are many non-human resources inside a classroom which, if well used, are crucial for learning. These are the many things which the teacher (and later the class members) can find themselves organising outside and beyond the face-to-face meetings of the community.

It's also the case that although a class may create rich and important learning experiences, it often benefits from wider links. One of the principles identified for learning communities has been described as the 'Beyond the Bounds Principle: the community should go beyond the knowledge in the community and seek out new approaches and ideas that challenge what they believe'.[1] As well as seeking out ideas, learning communities often seek out new contacts, and it may be useful to consider the web of contacts outside the classroom and how these can be most constructive. So this chapter will start with a view of the non-human resources within the classroom, but will go on to examine the resources outside the classroom.

In a classroom which runs as a learning community, the teacher's role is significantly more that of mobiliser of resources, rather than being the resource or the knowledge guardian.

Resources are one thing – access is another

For a learning community, probably just as important as the issue of what are the resources for learning which can be made available, is the issue of who has access to such resources (and feels enabled to do so). This point was brought home to me during a period when secondary school teachers were experimenting with 'flexible learning' in which students were given teacher-written resources, planned their route of learning, use of these resources, and so on. In that context one science teacher said to me that she had completely underestimated the impact of unlocking the previously locked cupboards in her lab. She was not creating a free-for-all, but was putting the tools for investigation into the hands of the investigators. Nowadays I am struck by a similar issue in relation to computers in classrooms. Especially in primary schools where the computers are more likely to be distributed around classrooms (rather than stuck in 'suites'!) I notice a very big difference across different classrooms. In some classrooms it is only the teacher who has hands on the keyboard/controls: in others I have seen, it was only the pupils.

So we might be well advised to keep in mind three questions:

* What are the resources?
* Do learners have access?
* Do they feel empowered to access them?

If the answer to these three is 'yes', then the classroom in question will have taken a major step in distributing the sources of learning away from solely the teacher, and into the classroom and wider environment.

Self and others as resource

The experience of too many learners in classrooms is one of not feeling a resource for themselves, let alone for their colleagues. The experience of enhancing agency and collaboration in a classroom changes this, in a way which is sometimes slow to start but then sometimes transformational. As learners start to find they have questions, can form these into enquiries, can lead rich and consequential investigations, and communicate their new knowledge, their view of learning and themselves as learners shifts towards seeing themselves as more resourceful.

As collaboration develops, so too may the sense that each learner is acting as a resource for their colleagues. But I use the word 'may' deliberately, because it is only dependable that this sense grows if a certain form of communication happens. It is the communication I have called collective reflection, in which everyone stops to review, in other words to exchange accounts of what they have noticed, understood, found helpful, and so on. It is in these exchanges that learners start to hear how they are a resource for each other, and unless they hear something of each other's experiences they may never get to know that. I have found some adults to have transforming surprises on such occasions. Their initial understanding of the community is, perhaps necessarily, framed in their own expectations and worldview. But when they hear the detailed experiences of a reasonably diverse range of others, such expectations are opened to revision. For a person who is regularly talkative, to hear that another finds great difficulty in contributing to discussion is perhaps a surprise, and to find that they can together help each others' learning development is a real example of seeing oneself in a new light as a resource to others.

Pupils who experience themselves as a resource to others have impressed me as having a sense of pride – of the best sort. I remember well visiting Robin Hood Primary school, a very learning-enriched environment, and at one point met a 10-year-old boy at a computer just off the classroom. He showed me the presentation he was just finishing, on society's attitudes towards refugees, and I found it moving. But he positively glowed when he interjected into our conversation, 'I'm a computer tutor'. This meant that he had become a resource for others when they needed advice on computer matters. Support sessions had been provided for this new role, in which he learned about how to draw out his colleagues' difficulties, and how best to offer help.

Peer learning, peer tutoring, peer mentoring, peer mediation – all these terms have in common the roles that pupils can play as a resource to each other, and plenty of evidence on their impact shows that with appropriate reflection and support they can be of great benefit to all the parties involved.

Material resources

Classrooms are full (sometimes over-full?) of objects which could be resources in learning. Many of these are texts – books and other materials. Such texts, and indeed those other objects and tools, can be seen as embodiments of the knowledge that earlier generations have packaged for the next. But knowledge is not simply 'passed on' through this process, and active methods for appropriating it – such as Reciprocal Teaching described in the previous chapter – help young people to be selective and constructive, thereby gaining core skills for the future that is theirs.

Classrooms and schools are sometimes more full of resources than are other places in their neighbourhood (witness their role as targets for theft), and the issue of 'access' to such resources has already been raised. But even for the material resources which surround pupils every day, I have sometimes been surprised at how pupils can act as though they were resource-starved. I remember a particular afternoon in Sonia's class of 8-year-olds when we were to be scientists and when the theme was shadows. In small groups pupils were first identifying interesting phenomena to do with shadows, then an investigation, with an emphasis on 'fair tests'. What struck me was that some of these young people were very highly interested to collect various materials from around the classroom and to examine shadow phenomena in relation to them. But they acted as though they had never used these materials before! Notwithstanding the idea that these were indeed new resources for the new issue at hand, I felt they were excited about being allowed access.

Resources and tools are, of course, only interesting to the extent that they serve a purpose. Remembering this helps us to avoid a few educational perils which accompany the ways of helping people to become more effective users of resources. The perils I am thinking of are well illustrated in the field of computer training, where examples such as government-funded training for teachers to use computers have been particularly poorly evaluated. From what I understand the reason is that such experiences focused on learning how to use the computer rather than on using the computer to do something of interest, importance and value. For me it seems to parallel the idea of teaching people about pens rather than helping them write.

All ICT tools such as computers, copiers, cameras and sound systems are just that: tools which relate to purpose. And when they find a role in relation to tasks which are both compositional and consequential the degree of engagement is high and skills are learned without being taught. Resources and tools then support productive agency in its best sense, that is creating products which embody and communicate the choices, decisions and priorities of their learning.

Knowledge-building software for communities: CSILE and Knowledge Forum

Many grandiose claims are made for the future of classrooms to be transformed by ICT. Such claims seem to imply that ICT defines the classroom, rather than being a tool in the classroom. Evidence on the uptake of ICT in classrooms challenges such a simple claim, and shows that ICT use depends on the view of pedagogy which is already operating in any classroom before ICT is introduced. As Larry Cuban put it: 'Computer meets classroom, classroom wins'.[2]

Much of the technology which is currently sold to classrooms is not designed for education at all: it is business software (word processing, graphics, presentation, video) which is an important potential tool in anyone's hands, but does not embody a design for learning. Much of what is sold as 'educational software' is built on a very limited conception of learning. In some cases pupils use computers to play supposedly educational versions of arcade games. Much of the time such technology reinforces the dominant and out-of-date view of classrooms and of learning.

But suitably designed ICT can make an important contribution to the operation of a classroom as a learning community, and there is one shining example which embodies sophisticated views of learning and knowledge, and which has now benefited from decades of research and development work. Its use spans North America, continental Europe and the Far East, and includes primary, secondary and higher education, healthcare, community and business contexts.

Originally called 'CSILE', each of the terms in that abbreviation are important: Computer Supported Intentional Learning Environments.

This technology aims to support the setting up of an environment which supports the intentional learning of a number of people. Such learners, individually or in combination, have access to computers on a network, and thus to the CSILE software (later versions also allow web access, but I will limit myself to classroom uses here). The software creates a networked community space in which learners can engage in the processes of building knowledge, and thereby create or improve community knowledge. This is a very different vision of ICT than that of sticking pupils in front of individual terminals, so it might be useful to bring to life the way in which CSILE, and its successor Knowledge Forum, operate.

CSILE fosters participation in a research-like process of enquiry by engaging students in a process of generating their own questions, setting up intuitive theories and searching information as well as sharing their cognitive achievements. Pupils contribute to this networked community space by two main methods: adding notes to a public-knowledge map, and adding contributions to a public discussion.

Figure 8.1 shows an example[3] of an opening discussion on the question 'How does heat affect solids?', which shows the contributions of different notes towards a learning dialogue. The system specifically provides for student collaboration by allowing students to compose notes

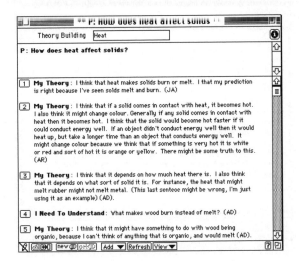

Figure 8.1 Example of discussion notes in CSILE

that are comments to other notes or link two existing notes. The starting stems for such notes are (with slight variations in different versions):

> *I think an explanation of this is:*
> *I need to understand:*
> *I have accessed New Information on:*
> *A better theory could be:*
> *Rising above this, I think:*
> *Putting our knowledge together:*

In such notes can be seen the prompts to promote enquiry, dialogue, synthesis and metacognition. Figure 8.2 gives an example of a 'rise-above' note. This example shows a student's high-level summary of knowledge advances over a period of several months.[4] This student packaged the set of notes that led to the discovery reported here; his older notes are now accessible only through this rise-above note. Rise-above notes are also used to synthesise ideas, create historical accounts and archives, reduce redundancy, and in other ways impose order on ideas.

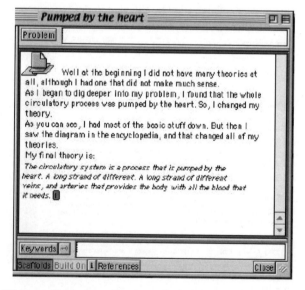

Figure 8.2 Example of a 'rise-above' note in CSILE/Knowledge Forum

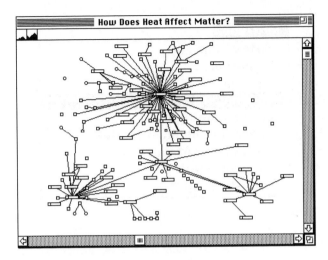

Figure 8.3 View of a web of notes in CSILE

As the enquiry and dialogue progress, so the community knowledge map becomes more complex. The cumulating collection of notes and contributions can be viewed to show the links that pupils are making between elements in their communal knowledge. Figure 8.3 shows discussions, graphics and notes, together with the links made.

As the communal web of notes develops, different ways of retrieving them from the database are available so that different analyses can be made and developments tracked. Figure 8.4 gives an example of the ways which are available to community members. When a student requests the 'Comments On All My Notes' view, she is supported toward collaborative communication with any other members of the community. This is also promoted when she logs onto the system and is notified of all of the comments made to her notes.

As nearly a dozen of the citations in Chapter 4 showed, the use of this software has contributed significantly for more than a decade to our understanding of the benefits of classrooms which operate as learning communities. Students ask higher-order questions, are engaged in more reflective activity, show higher self-regard and richer conceptions of learning, alongside significant improvement in problem-solving and recall of complex information. One other indicator is worth mentioning.

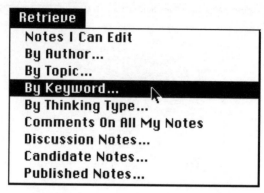

Figure 8.4 Ways of retrieving notes in CSILE

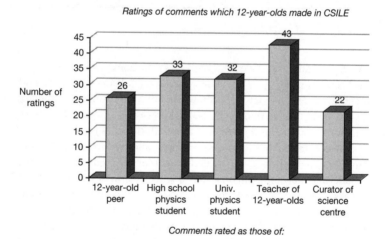

Figure 8.5 Quality of student notes in CSILE

A bank of 156 comments created in CSILE by 12-year-olds was shown to outside evaluators, who were asked to judge the level of the authors of these comments. As Figure 8.5[5] shows, only 17 per cent of comments were rated as written by students of this age: 83 per cent were rated high enough in quality as to be written by higher-level students, teachers or science professionals.

'Post-its™': a community resource

As was briefly mentioned in Chapter 4, the principles involved in CSILE can, to some extent, be achieved through more 'low-tech' methods. Mary Ann Van Tassell writes about using a wall-chart to display the ideas and questions her 6- and 7-year-old class posed on Air, and how this developed into further enquiries and further charts:

> As the students continued to conduct different experiments, our charts of 'What Air Does' and 'Things that Use Air' grew. These two charts, and the questions behind them, guided our initial investigation into air as we built the foundation. We would return to our charts after each experiment, and revise or add to them in light of newly acquired knowledge.[6]

Karen Hume also writes about scientific enquiry in her classroom, where the boards on two sides of the room are used in a new way:

> the board is frequently covered with a hundred or more yellow, fluorescent pink, and neon green 'post it™' notes, written by my class. . . . When students aren't posting their notes, they are engaged in a wide variety of related activities: reading the notes that are already posted; standing at the board and discussing the notes with others; or writing notes at their desks, based on reading, conversation, and experimentation, and then returning to post them to 'the wall'. That's what we call it – our knowledge building wall, and its development is the central activity in most of our inquiries.[7]

Emily a teacher in a north London school, describes how her practice of 'news-time' with her 6-year-olds was transformed by the introduction of the Post-it™.

I 'unpacked' with my class the reasons for news and what we want to happen during news time. We devised a set of guidelines based on the acronym of NEWS:

Nurture
Encourage
Wait and listen
Smile 'n' share

We came up with two aspects of News Time they wanted to change. First, they all wanted to 'share' in small groups about things that they have interest in. Second, they wanted to have it at a regular time each week.

We settled on a concept, based loosely on Hume's (2000) 'knowledge wall'. Students would write one sentence about their news on a Post-it™ note and stick it to the News Wall. The wall served as a focal point of the classroom. After all children had offered their news to the wall, one by one children would come and choose a Post-it™ note news idea that interested them. The children then formed interest groups and took turns to elaborate about their news. We decided that a limit of five minutes per news share was enough and if we felt we did not have enough time we would put a star in the corner to show that more time was needed. At the end of the session, we joint-constructed a summary of our news time, using the Post-its™ as a writing frame or plan.

Emily developed the practice with her class to include both 'true' news stories and 'imagined' news. Both contributed to community-building: 'true' stories created a rich historical account which constantly supported and expanded their development as a community. With regard to the fictional stories, 'Children shared news about overcoming difficulties, consequences of not doing as one was told and "magical or lucky" discoveries. News time became an allegorical journey of discovery.'

Others who have reviewed these practices[8] give accounts of their use in other domains. For example in helping a class of 6-year-olds bring together and relate their responses to reading particular literature. Each Post-it™ is called a 'seed', and the spatial relation which the class decides between them is called a 'web'. In the construction together, the richness of metacognitive talk develops. Here the act of writing and the possibilities of objectification which it brings are key steps in creating a communal object for further and deeper analysis, and importantly the object is always changeable.

In Sonia's classroom enquiries into class experiences of learning have encouraged reflection and meta-learning on a number of themes, each of which culminates with class members placing their Post-its™ on a class poster, headed for example, 'When I'm engaged . . . ', and 'I help myself become engaged by/when . . . '.

Bridging to wider worlds

There's something about the walls that often define a classroom which sometimes lead to the focus staying within the walls, and the apparent belief that it's only what happens within those walls which matters for learning. Such encapsulated classrooms, as with encapsulated schools, often display more difficulties reflecting the fact that this is not the healthiest way to be, for learning or for social relations.

There's something about the ideas in classrooms as learning communities which soon create a different picture. If knowledge-generation is the task and students use their classroom and school resources to the full, they may find that their enquiries lead them beyond the classroom walls. At such a moment, some degree of facilitating this process of bridging to wider worlds may be required. In the busy lives of most teachers, this may seem like an extra task which can be assigned to the category of a luxury, but when a teacher's role has made some shift towards that of mobiliser of resources, they may feel much more inclined to extend their repertoire in this way. Some accounts show how pupils go beyond the boundaries of school and go beyond the levels of achievement that schools expect: for example, a group of young learners whose enquiries soon exhausted the text resources available in their classroom and school, and who went on to make connections with local university staff and its library.[9]

At this point I think of another act of bridging which is all too seldom seen that way. It is the practice of allocating pupils 'homework', which all too often can comprise more of the same 'busy work' tasks that can characterise classroom life. Such a practice seems to ignore completely the resources which pupils have available to them outside the classroom: again these are human and material in a diverse range. A change to this pattern has been successfully achieved by many teachers, as a spin-off from changing the discourse of their classrooms. Those teachers who together with their classes set out to dispense with the word 'work' and see what happens when the word 'learning' is substituted find very energising results. When these extend to the change from setting 'homework' to suggesting 'home learning', the benefits widen. Parents find themselves more engaged, as a diversity in their contribution seems more possible: reviews of how different pupils in a class have managed their home learning give rise to talk about the very skills which all of us need in the wider world. Many pupils choose to do their home learning together. So we could transform homework into another contribution in each pupil's wider community learning, and through the process of review, support the development of a wider sense of the classroom community to make best use of the resources there.

Being like other communities

Back 'inside' the classroom, one last sense of the resource available to the class as a community is their sense of themselves as a knowledge-generating community, but two points need to be addressed for this to be a felt resource. The first is the importance of any classroom community generating knowledge of its processes through the practices of meta-learning: without this there is no reason to assume that community members would get to know that sense of themselves as a community resource. The second point is that there are multiple versions of this, and a multiple sense of this resource to achieve. Such possibilities are to be found when classroom practitioners invite a class to 'be' like scientists, or music-makers, or historians, or magazine-writers. As was mentioned in Chapter 5, these are invitations to learn the identities which accompany membership of particular knowledge communities, and can be particularly motivating. In some way these are modelled on what we all think we know about such knowledge communities, and as such they can engage more authentic processes than doing school science or textbook history or writing for the English teacher.

The advantage of there being multiple communities to become is that within the range there will be more opportunities for diverse members of the class to shine, as well as offering a more realistic miniature of non-school life.

However, the usual forces operate to make this achievement more difficult than it need be. As an example, in Sonia's class mentioned earlier, where we were 'being scientists', the issues of 'fair tests' was derived from the prescribed curriculum, rather than from the emergent knowledge of the class. Its effect was to short-cut some matters, thus undermining the process of the group by suggesting that there was some right answer or gold standard by which to judge their plans for experiment. Some writers see this regularly:

> Many attempts to model classrooms as science end up reverting to an individual focus (i.e. to what extent do children think and act as scientists) rather than a social one (i.e. to what extent does a school class function like a scientific community).[10]

So the challenge was to de-emphasise the prescribed curriculum, and instead to think about how a scientific community operates. This led to thinking about how scientists report their findings to each other, how they utilise peer review, how disputes are (or are not) settled, and so on. Perhaps the class could emulate a scientific conference at appropriate intervals, in order to learn about these processes. This would possibly reflect other examples which have found that children of this age rate most highly, for learning and for enjoyment, presenting their findings to each other.[11]

I use the term 'emulate' rather than 'simulate' in order to avoid any connotation that this is game-playing rather than aspirational action. There is a degree of scepticism about whether the activity outlined above can be described as 'really doing science'. I take the view that it can, and see no reason to denigrate it because it may have some novice status. I concur with the view that school-age students

> can begin functioning as real scientists as soon as they are able to engage in a form of practice that is authentically scientific, one that is concerned with the solution of recognizably scientific problems in recognizably scientific ways. Analogous arguments can be made about authentic functioning in history, literature and other disciplines that students may venture into in their knowledge-building efforts.[12]

Learning about networks

I suppose that the point just made about acting like a community of scientists and emulating how their networks operate takes us to the furthest reaches of what a classroom learning community can offer, in that if it promotes access to a wider network it should also promote learning about wider networks. There are other current examples, particularly those in which classes of students in different countries set up e-mail or web-based communication between them, and for some period of time build knowledge of each other through such networks. These initiatives are bound to come and go, but may also lead to long-standing links for some individuals, and learning about all this through reviewing it seems of value.

As this chapter ends, have new issues about resources in your classroom come to mind? And about learners' access to them? And their feeling of being empowered to access? If the classroom promotes resourcefulness and the sense of community as resource, learner engagement is likely to be high.

In the management of all this, and the final aspect of the activity systems of classrooms as learning communities, we now turn to consider roles.

Prompts for reflection

- Think about the access to resources which learners exercise in your class. What messages about their trustworthiness as learners are being conveyed?
- Do learners in your class feel that they are a resource for each other's learning? What sorts of activities might help them feel this more and exercise it more?
- Particular resources have been introduced in this chapter: CSILE/Knowledge Forum, Post-it™ notes, resources beyond the classroom walls. Have these interested you enough to develop a plan for experimenting with them (adapting as you go, of course)?

9 Roles in a learning community

Whose job is it to do what to/with/for whom in a learning community? The issues discussed in this chapter address the central matter of new roles in the classroom, and are sometimes the issues which teachers report feeling most keenly.

Community governance

To start off our consideration of the governance in a learning community, let's examine some examples which test the concept quite severely. By this I mean examples where there is concern about a class and this concern comes in the form of the behaviour in the class. On such occasions, the stock responses in schools are teacher-centred and predominantly reactive, as summed up with phrases such as 'dealing with a difficult class'. As I have discussed elsewhere,[1] these stock responses are often 'more of the same' and do not have positive benefits in the long term.

Jack is a teacher in a north London school, and writes about his experience of being asked to work with a disaffected class of 16-year-olds. Jack has heard the perspective of the class's teacher in the previous year, who:

> felt that their behaviour was extremely hard to deal with, despite his frequent use of the school Assertive Discipline Behaviour policy . . .
>
> He described the noise level as being a real concern, as well as refusal to 'pay attention' to him. He had sent many students out

to work with other teachers during the year, and three were permanently removed to join another class taught by an assistant headteacher. Numerous letters were sent home to families about the behaviour of students during lessons. The teacher had spent an enormous amount of time writing letters, dealing with students who he saw as not listening and stopping the lesson from proceeding as he had wished. . . . The teacher had begun to view the students as a group, almost a unitary force in opposition to himself.

What does Jack do? The first thing in working with the class was to elicit the student perspective. In this case it was done through a brief written enquiry. Responses like the following were collected:

I can't say I was satisfied with the education given to us in year 10. This may be because the classroom wasn't organised well, we couldn't work with others because of the teacher and students shouting at each other constantly.

(Hasan)

There was no sort of communication or relationship between the students and the teacher. The atmosphere was chaotic, we could argue with the teacher and walk out as we pleased. Our thoughts weren't considered so in return we didn't consider his.

(Sarah)

Class responses demonstrated that the class were tuned in to matters of relationship, and that they did not want the current situation to continue. At the same time, Jack noticed that students had been taking home the classwork they were not completing in class. Noticing this may have been especially helpful for Jack in that he did not fall into the stance which is often voiced in school staffrooms: 'This lot just don't want to learn'. Having avoided this attribution Jack's stance was to focus on learning, not behaviour, and to again elicit student views:

We asked the students to decide on what conditions would best suit their own needs to be successful learners. The group came to some decisions which were presented as a set of rules we all agreed to follow. . . . The new rules were printed up as a poster on the classroom wall:

❏ Everyone to concentrate and get better grades
❏ Enough space – not squashed together
❏ Background music
❏ Encouragement from teachers – not pressure
❏ Access to computers and the library
❏ Help from classmates
❏ Permission to move around to help others
❏ Relaxed atmosphere – not too loud
❏ Wait your turn to see teacher – be patient
❏ Individuals to get attention from both teachers
❏ Don't waste time or take advantage

Both of the steps in Jack's account give us examples of community governance. That's not an easy phrase but it indicates important messages such as:

– Your voice is important.
– It's more important as a worked-through collective.
   Learning is the important goal here.
– You can take a share in making things better.

These are messages which the vast majority of pupils in our schools take ahead constructively. For the purpose of this chapter, it may be worth noting that in these examples there had not been a lot of community-building work in place before these governance approaches were used. So it's not as though they are processes which only exist when a collective has become a community. Indeed they may be important contributors to the building of community.

But a key message (which can be emphasised at any time, and which is more effective when re-emphasised) is that it is important to have a vision of classroom as community when addressing difficulty. This was present in Siân's account of her experience with a class of 11-year-olds in an east London school. Siân is teaching music in an active way, but this class has not developed productive agency. And the class has not developed any social cohesion. As Siân explains, this was:

a class in which there were disparate small groups of friends . . . also a number of students who did not fit into any of the established friendship groups. There was little positive communication between the separate groups and normally a good deal of tension, often erupting in verbal and sometimes physical abuse.

A pattern emerged – lessons often broke down. . . . The habitual, punitive approaches such as detentions and talking to parents were totally inadequate; any effect these strategies may once have had in encouraging individuals in 7E to comply with the school's classroom code had long worn off.

Instead, I worked my way through a range of learning strategies, . . . and whilst these strategies had some effect, I felt that I was skirting the fundamental issues – the negative relationships both between the students and between them and me. . . . I knew that 7E and I needed to agree a common approach to enable what everyone actually wanted to happen, turning 'I' and 'they' into 'we'.

That vision of what was needed and what it would lead to was crucial to the intervention which Siân arranged. For one lesson a discussion on 'what we want from this class' was arranged.

I was not confident that I could run a discussion session with 7E along these lines without enlisting some help. In this instance, help came in the form of a senior member of staff who did not teach the class but had been in the school a number of years and had gained the respect of students and staff alike. I talked the problem through with her and we agreed that she should come in as a neutral observer whose presence would have a calming effect on the students in 7E.

The resulting discussion was not easy, and neither was the route that followed, because it was a two-way process in which everyone had to compromise.

7E and I did manage to establish a relationship where collaborative work became a regular part of lessons and sessions where sharing of work took place became more supportive. Discussions around mutual respect reoccurred throughout our lessons over the next academic year and there was constant fluctuation along the scale of 'I' and 'they' to 'we'. What was most significant was that a vocabulary to discuss our relationship was introduced and that channels of communication were opened; consequently the fundamental issue of learning relationships was at least partially addressed.

Siân's story reminds me of the importance of voicing a vision. It does not suggest that voicing a vision is all that is needed to achieve that vision: compromise and working together need time. But having voiced something about community governance, it is possible to return to it, in whatever form of language has been appropriate for a particular class. Certainly Siân's scale of 'I' and 'they' to 'we' is one on which classrooms vary considerably, but the language of 'we' is crucial in indicating a more community-based vision for the class.

Starting with learning

These two starting examples give an introduction to some of the possibilities and some of the advantages of community governance when there is a concern about behaviour. I have argued elsewhere[2] that asking 'How can I help the classroom become an environment in which behaviour difficulties don't arise?' leads to equally immediate action as when we ask 'How will I respond to that incident?'. The difference between the two questions is one of scale but not of immediacy, and the matter of scale is important for the title of this chapter because community governance carries the message that we all have a role in improving this. As a contribution to managing classroom behaviour, building classroom community goes well beyond those methods which seem designed to produce compliance,[3] and helps to achieve many of the wider and important goals of school.

Some of the methods which further contribute to this development include:

- class meetings, perhaps using a circle time or other appropriate methodology, to achieve new tasks and arrange events for the class;
- class reviews, which specifically address how the community feels and what would improve its working;
- class problem-solving that addresses issues which arise, and through its workings creates more effective solutions at the same time as building agency.

An underlying theme to these methods is that of regularly asking 'What sort of classroom do we want?', and following through with the responsibilities which we take on in order to achieve the things we want. The teacher can feel challenged at times by really taking on class ideas which he or she may not have chosen. The teacher will also have to challenge any community outcomes which are not genuine solutions, for example false compromises or subtle bargains.

But, as Jack's example above showed, even if we read a classroom situation as one with behaviour concerns, we can very usefully start the community governance with a focus on learning.

The example given of Juliet's class (end of Chapter 5) indicates how such a stance may develop into a clear and public statement of a class of 10-year-olds' view of a learning community. Juliet's example leads to a further point: the fact that the principles were displayed at the classroom door, and were for action by everyone, created a *public* statement of the community – something for all to see and perhaps to refer to.

Community needs a public presence

Evidence that classrooms are populated by communities is more unusual than at first might be thought. Just look at classrooms you know or classrooms you have known, and ask yourself what messages were there which represented the fact that a community of learners inhabited that space. Plenty of teacher things. Plenty of individual learner products. What about the collective?

In primary schools I sometimes see photographs of the class on a special event, or some statements by the class on when their learning is best, or a poster made out of each class member's comments on something (in such examples the key resource for public community statements is often present – the Post-it™ note). Sometimes I see public presence for the fact that this community relates to others around it, as for example when a class noticeboard collects members' ideas for discussion at the next school council meeting.

In secondary schools, especially those in which pupils spend amounts of their day changing rooms, there is often less public evidence of classroom communities. But a moment's thought brings this into question. Why might we not see some of 9R's hopes for their chemistry learning publicised in the same room as 11G's? Indeed, may it not lead to some new possibilities of communication between them? Can we imagine a notice: 'We are trying to improve our understanding of diffusion and would welcome talking with anyone else about this, beyond the time Ms Stevenson can give us. (signed) 9R'.

Changes in role are changes in relationship

Although those with a bureaucratic turn of mind try to portray roles as though they were lists of duties, the reality doesn't turn out like the lists. A major part of the reason for this is that roles cannot be defined on their own. Just try to think of any role term, and you will find that you also have to think of another role – what is called the role partner. For example: mother–child. Even the hermit organises him/herself in relation to the rest of the world. So it is not sensible to think of a teacher without thinking also of the pupils, and this affirms the long-standing recognition of teachers that they cannot enact their desired role if pupils do not go along with it.

So what is a role, in this view? It is a meaningful bundle of interactions with your role partners. It has to make meaning to you for a start (remember those doubts about can I be a teacher?), and then can be made meaningful in interaction with pupils you meet. It's much more flexible than a list of duties (or a list of 'competences' to be displayed!).

If we take this seriously, it offers a very important ally to teachers who are making the shift from the dominant teacher-centred view of their role towards a more learner-centred one. For it indicates that pupils are likely to go along with such a change – although it will be unusual at first and therefore runs the risk of generating 'resistance' – if it is well explained and worked out with them (which it necessarily had to be anyway).

So just imagine how you might explain to pupils you know the various aspects of your change towards a more learner-centred and collaborative classroom environment. I think you might find that explanations make a considerable amount of sense to you and (with time for adjustment) to your pupils. Examples which go through my mind include:

- *'The curriculum is for you to cover, and I'm here to help you.'*
- *'I want to organise things around your questions so that you'll be more engaged.'*

- *'It won't always feel easy to do this if we're not used to it.'*
- *'I'd like to hear how you can best help each other to learn that.'*
- *'I think what you say to yourself is more influential than anything I say to you.'*
- *'I'm more interested in your view rather than my summary so I want you to read it for yourselves.'*
- *'If you think well, you'll do well.'*
- *'I'm interested in your examples where you know this idea is used, and some examples you can imagine it being used.'*
- *'I want you to demonstrate how good you are at this, not me show you how good I am!'*
- *'When I'm not here, what will you do?'*
- *'I'd like you to think of a way you can evaluate yourselves on that.'*

What's noticeable about these examples is that they often contain reference to both 'I' and 'you'. In that way they may be an improvement on things we say which contain only one of those – 'I want . . . ' and 'You must . . . '. This shift, even on its own, could have an important impact on the relationships in the classroom, since it carries a relational message rather than an authority message. And if it is accompanied by changes in tasks, social structure and so on, then it is likely to form an important contribution to the 'we' language which is our goal.

Changes in role for the teacher

Becoming learner-centred is quite a challenge, when you take seriously the powerful messages in school and society which maintain the dominant teacher-centred view. So what can we anticipate in this change, including the dynamics which might delay or divert it?

Maryellen Weimer[4] identifies seven areas of change when developing learner-centred classrooms:

1 Teachers do classroom tasks less. They assign to students some of the tasks: organising the content, and so on.
2 Teachers do less telling; students do more discovering.
3 Teachers do more design work. They design activities to help pupils advance, do the work of practitioners in the discipline, and develop reflection about their learning.

4 Staff do more modelling. Demonstrate how a skilled learner (the teacher) continues to learn.
5 Staff do more to get students learning from and with each other. Create work for small groups to do in class.
6 Staff work to create climates for learning, one that promotes interaction, autonomy and responsibility.
7 Staff use other means of gaining feedback rather than merely mark work.

What I find interesting about these seven areas of shift in classroom relationships is the voices they set off in practitioners who attempt them. It should not surprise us that the dominant voices in our society reside in everyone's head, and it is on these occasions that they pop out to keep the situation in the status quo. The exchanges that are imaginable always bring in a conservative voice. For example:

- *'I want you to be organising how the content will be covered.'*
- *'But that's your job – and you're paid for it!'*

or

- *'I'd like to hear how you can best help each other to learn that.'*
- *'It would be better if you told us.'*

or

- *'I'd like you to think of a way you can evaluate yourselves on that.'*
- *'But you're meant to know the right answers.'*

In these unspoken interchanges hangs the balance of change. I sometimes hear teachers voicing these comments of the (imagined) pupil as reasons why they should not experiment. This is a fascinating version of who has responsibility for what! Those teachers who move on, to consider how they may respond to each of the imagined conservative voices, and even practise how to respond, are open to learning and change in their classrooms.

On occasion, other voices pop out to maintain the status quo – as in this lovely example from Anne in one of my classes:

It feels strange to be embarking on this when the 'teacher' has not made the learning objectives explicit, nor does the 'class' know what the expected outcome is to be. An Ofsted inspector in the classroom might take a dim view of this.

(Learning Log 11.5.04)

How accurate that is! A dim view in the sense that viewing a learning community through the lenses of the Ofsted inspection framework does not give much illumination at all! (see interlude on observing classrooms following this chapter). But the feeling of strangeness was not sufficient to stop us continuing, and this was helped by knowing that an Ofsted-style visitor would be operating with a view of learning much more reduced than the one we were building.

But perhaps most insightful is the understanding which emerges from Alyson's account of operating her Chemistry class of 12/13-year-olds as a learning community. Here she noticed that the voice which was sometimes most difficult to handle was her own, in the sense that her own view of her role as a teacher was brought into sharp relief during the development of this classroom practice. In the later stages of a sequence of only eight weeks, with one of her less favourite classes and least favourite topics, Alyson says:

Wherever possible I encouraged and offered advice about the next steps, and even considered resorting to a traditional method of teaching. In the end, though, I just let them get on with it. I felt that if we were really to learn anything from this experience I had to let the students discover the problems and solve them for themselves. The lack of control I allowed myself at that time was frightening! I had learnt that if I wanted my students to take responsibility for their own learning then I had to be prepared to let them have that responsibility.

We will read more about Alyson's observations of the pupils in that class shortly.

Changes in role for the pupils

I have noted in the section above the way that a pupil voice might be called upon by a teacher as a reason for not making change. Beyond that there are real occasions when pupils show us that being in a learning community is initially uncomfortable for the way they have been socialised to date. This phenomenon also occurs in my work with adults, and (especially in the early stages) I attempt to inoculate participants against negative effects by offering ideas such as:

> As the process we are proposing is not the dominant one in teaching and learning, we may at first feel uncomfortable or puzzled. Whatever happens, let's aim to learn from it.

Nevertheless, people still experience unease in their changed and changing roles, as voiced by Cynthia:

> . . . a feeling of slight apprehension that Chris is no longer going to 'teach', that we have to do the rest on our own – how much more would students feel this . . . [?]

> (Learning Journal 25.5.04)

I have no definitive list of experiences to offer for what pupils will feel in all situations of building a learning community. Indeed I am struck at the difference between the reports from different contexts. But there are three broad themes which it might be possible to anticipate, as they highlight the nature of life in the dominant classroom. On the three themes of changing strategies, changing responsibilities and changing routines we might not be surprised if pupils experienced and expressed some unease.

Changing strategies

The socialisation of the dominant classroom leads most pupils to act strategically – how can I get the best individual result (or the least chance of shame) with the most economical use of effort? So pupils who are introduced to learning communities may take a while to overcome the attitude of 'it's more work this way' before they allow themselves to experience learning instead of work and commitment instead of passivity.

Changing responsibilities

In the dominant classroom teacher is right and teacher decides the agenda. The dynamic of 'What's the right answer, miss?' has a long history in our schools, and it may even have strengthened in recent years. So pupils moving from 'right answers' to following their own important enquiries may initially need support in trusting their own questions. If the first step in changing responsibilities is from teacher to pupil, the second step is from individual to shared pupil responsibility. This theme is highlighted in the example of assessment, especially if there is some form of collaborative assessment. On such occasions students of all ages can feel particularly challenged: their internal voices are saying things which hark back to their major experience of individualised assessment, such as 'but where will *my* grade be?' and 'If I'm working with others for a group product, what happens if one of them is useless?'. I experience these themes when asking of a course group of twenty or so experienced teachers that they create a community product for the course 'Building Learning Communities'. The ripples at this request are often stronger than I would have expected. But some time later people have developed a real sense of community and surprise themselves at the quality which their collaboration creates.

Changing routines

Complex situations like a classroom will usually develop routines to pattern their progress: the question is where do the routines come from and what type are they? Most classrooms operate on the predictable teacher-centred routines of old, so building new ones for a classroom to operate as a learning community may be disorienting at first.

I hope that the three themes discussed above have not generated the idea that the changes are daunting or difficult. In my experience of a range of teachers they are often a lot less than teachers anticipate. And the change of role for students is taken up with gusto. Here's Alyson again, who had to coin a new concept for her Chemistry class behaviour – over-engagement!

> . . . the students were more engaged with their learning than was normal. In fact it would be true to say that they were almost over-engaged with their learning! So much so that they were

ignoring me and were irritated by my interruptions aimed at re-directing them. I believe that they felt that I had handed responsibility for their learning to them and then kept shortening their learning time with my interruptions. This explanation would account for my students' irritation with me and their persistence with the tasks. Alternatively they were sensing my lack of control and were taking advantage of the situation in refusing to listen to my instructions. Given how challenging I had previously found the behaviour of this class this is a distinct possibility.

In Alyson's example, the time given to reflect on the process of learning was not a marked feature of this rushed experience. Perhaps a little more of that was already a feature of the environment in Kirsten's example. In her south London comprehensive school, she decided to run her year 9 History class in a different way. For just eight lessons over four weeks:

I posed the group the intended challenge; to create community knowledge and understanding of how life has changed for black Americans from the 1950s to 2004 and to create an end product which will enhance the knowledge and understanding of others.

Even for such a short period the change in student role was significant, and the pupils' reflections indicate rich learning.

1   *Do you feel this class has become a learning community as we have completed this project? Why?*

   'Yes, because we have all worked together to complete the same piece of work. We usually complete tasks individually and are expected to have something to show for ourselves at the end of a lesson. This was good because everyone did something and we did it together.'

   'My smaller group worked really well together and we learned a lot so yeah, I guess we have been a sort of community.'

2 *Which moments have helped you to advance your knowledge and understanding of the way you learn best?*

'Ms Timbrell usually helps us learn a lot, but with this project it was different. A lot of the time I didn't even notice she was there. This has helped me learn that I don't need someone telling me what to do to learn well.'

'The small group I was working in didn't really have any of my friends in it. By working with these other people, I have learned that it doesn't matter if you like someone or not, you can still learn from them. It has made me feel more open about listening to other people and other teachers I don't usually like.'

3 *What have you learned?*

'I have learned that when you have a challenge, you don't need to rush it and that you might have to change your ideas as you go along and work with others.'

'I have learned that we all have different thoughts and that by talking about them, you can learn a lot.'

Pupil roles – allocated or emergent?

The literature on group learning has many proposals for allocating roles to different members of a small group. At the simplest, a leader is appointed – and in the classroom context, it is usually the teacher who does the appointing. In other examples, a range of roles which are deemed to be key, for example, chair, time-keeper and scribe, are allocated. Alternatively, with more of an eye for group process, chair, recorder and facilitator can be appointed. Yet another possibility is for such roles to be suggested and for the group to decide which members will take each role.

Whichever version of allocation is used, there are often useful outcomes, in terms of helping a group to operate successfully. But I have a slight hesitation, since the group may not have learned much about the process of its success, and could end up with what is essentially a bureaucratic learning – if there's a problem, throw a role at it. Moreover, the role-learning is restricted to those group members who were allocated, rather than important role learning being available to all.

So I have a slight personal preference for the other alternative, which is to allow a variety of informal roles to emerge as the life of the group progresses, and have the group review this as one part of reviewing how well it is functioning for the achievement of its goals. My experience is that roles and role labels are not usually a high focus in such reviews, but matters of communication are – together with the developing trust to raise such matters with peers.

Teacher as public learner

One of the steps for teachers who move beyond that of leading a classroom community to leading a classroom learning community is to publicly present themselves as a learner. Numbers of teacher colleagues when hearing about this at first have remarked, 'But I honestly don't know whether I am learning', and when they go on to describe their school contexts as promoting compliance and lacking in reflection I can understand what they mean. But they and many other colleagues find that in their classroom, presenting themselves as a learner means small-scale actions which grow:

- remarking on what you notice – about the classroom, about learners, about yourself;
- talk aloud as you solve a problem, thereby revealing and modelling your thinking;
- talking about your response to ideas and how you learned the things which are now on the pupils' learning agenda;
- talking about any of your learning in other domains of life.

For teachers who are also students there is an extra potential for mentioning to class members aspects of your experience as a learner. This example from Naheeda was supported by the use of learning logs, both the class and her own. She writes:

> Revealing myself as a learner was an important part of the journey toward developing richer conceptions of learning. The journals were therefore an opportunity for the learners in my class to see and understand I was a learner. This was a powerful part of the dialogue

which ensued after journal writing. I would at times talk about my learning struggles. I can see in my own mind how aghast some of the learners were when I said that I felt I couldn't write my essay.

They responded with: '*But you are a teacher*'.

I then explained I was also a learner and learning was a struggle but that I just kept trying and even when things were foggy I just did not give up. I explained how talking to my tutor or peers helped me to understand and gave me the confidence to keep trying. This dialogue about myself as a learner is an important part of the way the journals happen in my class.

Leading the culture

There is obviously an important role for the teacher in leading the culture of a classroom which operates as a learning community. This function of bringing meaning to the various activities has been seen as the highest aspect of leadership, and can be exercised proactively while other more 'practical' functions are distributed amongst the class. For teachers to lead a culture of a learning community, they must have at least some faith or confidence in its possibilities. This is never complete, and to wait for it to be so before starting would be a sure-fire way of never starting at all. But once started it grows with confirmatory experience of what learners are enabled to do.

Culture is a high-level concept, not a behavioural one, so it is not possible to define everything in advance. But a sufficient sense of predictability is achieved through voicing the goals and making sense of the experiences. As one writer put it: 'Teachers establish a learning atmosphere that is predictable yet full of choices'.[5]

Given the 'against the grain' nature of the enterprise, it would be no surprise for teachers who lead this culture to find themselves, at first, leading those practical activities which are not part of the dominant experience of classrooms – for the pupils or for them. So activities such as collective reflection and learning logs are likely to be ones where teacher practical action makes a significant contribution to the culture shift in the classroom.

At such moments, doubts will perhaps be experienced, doubts which are voiced in the dominant discourse. Colleagues will perhaps hear that voice saying 'what will anyone looking in this classroom think about your performance as a teacher?', and in that voice all the dominant elements of observing and judging teacher performance arise. I experience that voice when my colleagues join me in the class, and have found myself noting in my learning log, 'It's interesting having colleague observers in the room: I find myself thinking about whether they approve of my role'. Again the theme of judgement and approval emerges.

Leading a culture means acting with confidence. Although the term 'confidence' is a problematic one when one person (often erroneously) attributes it to another, I take it to describe those occasions when we continue to act according to our principles while in the presence of the voice of fear. That voice may not go away completely, but to continue to act is crucial.

Principle-centred leadership is most appropriate for building the culture which captures those hallmarks of community – agency, belonging, cohesion, diversity. In the case of classrooms and learning it also turns out to be less of an effort than some colleagues may predict, reflecting that there are trustable forces being garnered when a learning community is built. As Kirsten put it:

> As I reflected upon and analysed the progress of the learning community in my diary, week-upon-week, I realised that the principles I had set out to adhere to were occurring naturally within the context of the project without too much effort on my part.

Leading other leaders

The very term 'leadership' comes with a bundle of everyday connotations; for example, that there is one leader, or that successful leadership behaviour can be specified. Both of these are challenged by evidence. There are always multiple leaders in any classroom collective, and operating as a community aims to engage and develop this rather than find it a problem.

Even in a context where there is control over the curriculum, teachers can engage pupils as planners. Zoe Donoahue[6] describes how a class of 10-year-olds reviewed and rated the different learning activities in their science unit on sound, and went on to contribute to the planning of the next unit. Such activity was very rich in promoting metacognition – through rating each activity for its learning and its enjoyment – as well as giving a good example of how teacher leadership could be distributed with good effect. Those who fear that such a proposal is tantamount to giving away the teacher's role might note that the pupils planned in teacher-directed lessons and rated them high for learning – though low for enjoyment. Most highly rated on both criteria were doing research and giving presentations.

Conclusion

At the close of this chapter, we conclude the analysis of facets of the activity systems which comprise classrooms as learning communities. For the final chapter we move from the goal of creating classroom learning communities to consider creating school-wide learning communities. There will be no quick fix. As one researcher put it in 1992: 'Figuring out how to accomplish these two goals is a task which could engage the productive energies of teachers and researchers well into the next century'.[7] That same writer proposed that in the journey this book is mapping: 'The criteria for judging teacher effectiveness shifts from that of delivering good lessons to that of being able to build or create a classroom learning community'. So before moving to consider the school, a moment on observing classrooms and, by implication, teachers' roles, is next.

Prompts for reflection

- The themes of this chapter have always been connected: community governance, community presence in the classroom, the shift of roles and relationships, new scripts for classroom practice, teachers as learners, and leading a distributed culture. They amount to a more healthy responsibility for both teachers and pupils.
- What experiences in classrooms have you had when the responsibilities for learning were healthily distributed? How did they come about, and what did you contribute?
- Even though you may be subject to various pressures, how can you help yourself to take practical steps towards promoting such a picture now?

Interlude

Observing classrooms as learning communities

At this point we are making the transition between chapters on classroom life (5 to 9) written mainly to the classroom teacher, and a final chapter on the school, written with a wider set of participants in mind. It's the sort of point where some distilling might be valuable, especially if it also addresses a crucial issue when others are brought into the picture – that of observation.

Observation is an interesting hobby, but not always a great way to achieve understanding. Observation of classrooms is especially challenging, since their complexity makes discerning the most meaningful aspects pretty problematic. This is especially the case if the observer is 'external to the classroom', a matter which researchers have grappled with for decades. Given this difficulty, observation is most often handled in a way which simplifies the complexities of classroom life, and in the process reverts to the dominant discourse.

The phenomenon can be demonstrated quite easily. Ask a group of colleague teachers to watch a videotape of a classroom for a few minutes, without giving them a particular framework for viewing. Then ask them to talk to each other about what they have seen. The comments they make will (often around 75 per cent of the time) do two things:

1 focus on the teacher;
2 focus on the negative.

There will be few comments about the classroom situation, the patterns of interactions between pupils, or indeed the pupils' roles as learners. The comments will be about what the teacher in the video did *not* do. This is the phenomenon of the 'hostile witness'. In UK schools it may have increased over the last decade as in the face of a broadly hostile inspection system, schools have imported into their own practices the practice of peers inspecting 'teacher performance'.

I regard it as a sad state of affairs because it leads to reduced forms of relationship between colleague teachers in a school (anyone can come in and judge me now), and reduced forms of learning. Indeed it leads to strategic defensiveness between colleagues, which is well portrayed in this cartoon which was given to me by a school in Hackney:

'Yes, of course you can observe me teaching.
Come on Monday morning when it's silent reading.'

Such observation also leads to a greatly reduced focus on the real processes which lead to learning in classrooms. As Terry Wrigley put it:

> A public discourse has been established which accounts for success-ful teaching in mechanistic and superficial terms as a set of external behaviours which are not linked to an understanding of learning. It is based on teacher performance, not interaction between teachers and learners.[1]

Observation in classrooms can be better than this. As Judith Warren Little says: 'Teachers welcome observation and profit from qualified observers who will not waste the teacher's time, who will not insult the teacher's intelligence, and who will work as hard to understand classroom events as the teachers do to conduct them'.[2] To achieve this, two changes are required: observers need to shift their focus of observation (as will be elaborated below), and observers need to shift their role, from that of roving judge to one of learning collaborator.

I have written elsewhere[3] about expanding the focus of observation from teacher to classroom, but here I want to propose what an observer might be able to see in a classroom operating as a learning community. In the process I will also contrast what can be seen from this perspective to the other ways of viewing which are based on other conceptions of learning.

The first is currently dominant in the official voice of inspection and has led to the situation I outlined at the start of this section. It is abbreviated from the Ofsted (2003) Inspection framework.[4]

Observing from the Transmission model: 'Learning = being taught':

- Teachers show good command of subjects.
- Teachers plan effectively.
- Teachers have clear learning objectives.
- Teachers interest pupils.
- Teachers make effective use of time.
- Students acquire new knowledge or skills in their work.
- Students show positive response to teaching.
- Students show engagement and concentration, and are productive.
- Teachers assess pupils' work thoroughly and constructively.
- Teachers use assessment to inform their planning and target-setting.
- Students understand how well they are doing and how they can improve.

As the words make clear, this perspective leads to a focus on teachers more than learners, views curriculum as delivering a body of knowledge, values tangible products and de-emphasises the social dimensions of learning and social outcomes of learning. As in the Ofsted inspection framework, quality of learning is viewed as a response to teaching.

The second perspective is abbreviated from research sponsored by the Bill Gates Foundation.[5]

Observing from the Construction model: 'Learning = individual sense-making':

- Students are engaged in active participation, exploration and research.
- Students are engaged in activities to develop understanding and create personal meaning through reflection.
- Student work shows evidence of conceptual understanding, not just recall.
- Students apply knowledge in real-world contexts.
- Students are presented with a challenging curriculum designed to develop depth of understanding.
- Teacher uses diverse experiences of students to build effective learning.
- Students are asked by the teacher to think about how they learn, explain how they solve problems, think about their difficulties in learning, think about how they could become better learners, try new ways of learning.[6]
- Assessment tasks are performances of understanding, based on higher-order thinking.

Again, the words make clear that the major focus of attention from this perspective is the students, their activity and meaning-making processes. Curriculum is more about big ideas and depth of understanding. Quality of learning is viewed as conceptual development, metacognition may be highlighted, and application is valued. But there is little explicit mention of collaboration, and the classroom may still be a collective of individual learners rather than a community.

The third perspective is abbreviated from preceding chapters of this book:

Observing from the Co-construction model: 'Learning = creating knowledge as part of doing things with others':

- Students operate together to improve knowledge.
- Students help each other learn through dialogue.
- Learning goals emerge and develop during enquiry.
- Students create products for each other and for others.
- Students access resources outside the class community.
- Students review how best the community supports learning.
- Students show understanding of how group processes promote their learning.
- The classroom social structures promote interdependence.
- Students display communal responsibility including in the governance of the classroom.
- Assessment tasks are community products which demonstrate increased complexity and a rich web of ideas.

This perspective focuses on social and collaborative processes, and views curriculum as a process of building and testing knowledge as a way of entering a language community. Quality of learning is seen in the quality of action and dialogue for improving community knowledge, and is seen as a distributed process in which all are involved.

In the context where you work and learn, try to find ways of observing from these different perspectives. As you try adopting the standpoint of each in turn (and grapple with the initial strangeness of the latter two), try to notice the impact that each perspective has:

- on what you observe;
- on what you see as learning;
- on your relationships with the teacher in the class;
- on your relationship with the pupils in the class.

10 Schools as learning communities

In this chapter I aim to consider some of the practices and principles which would need to be in place in a school so that classrooms may best operate as learning communities. The relationship between school issues and classroom issues will always be complex, so no simple prescriptions will be on offer. Some of the elements may be valued and valuable in any school, whether or not classrooms are being developed as communities, and by contrast their absence does not necessarily preclude a particular classroom developing as a learning community along the lines of the preceding five chapters.

Prevalent assumptions about schools as organisations may prove hazardous again, as identified in Chapter 3. There is no need to view schools as machines. Instead we need to consider how we would like our schools to be so that classrooms can become their best.

And the belief that schools are too difficult to change must be put aside. Schools are not some sort of monolith. There are more variations between schools than many teachers are aware of, including on dimensions which have significant impact on the themes of this book.

'You couldn't do that in the school I'm at'

When talking with teachers about change in their classrooms, their school as an organisation often comes into the picture. But sometimes it is presented as a major constraint on a teacher's capacity to experiment with effective learning in classrooms. Now I do not deny that there are some schools which act in a deeply controlling manner and demand compliance from their staff in a way which is inimical to learning, but

I think these are small in number. So this image of schools is more widespread than it should be, and reflects another phenomenon – the general disempowerment of teachers by politicians and schools, and perhaps the general cautious response to suggestions for change. Perhaps too it represents the dominant yet dubious mental model of organisations – that hierarchical power is strong – or even an element of self-protection – the comfort of being able to hold someone else, namely 'management', responsible for the lack of change. All these phenomena are about the low levels of agency which teachers experience in their profession, and just as agency was noted as a hallmark of classroom communities, so for schools.

The idea that the school limits the classroom is a real shame, because increasing evidence points to the fact that the classroom is much more important than the school for the key purpose of pupils' learning. In research on 'School Effectiveness', it has been recognised that classrooms have a major impact on the measured performance of pupils, and explain much more of the variation in performance data than do schools:

> The differences among classes within the same school are many times higher than differences between schools, indicating a high variability in teacher/class effectiveness.[1]

> Recent research on the impact of schools on student learning leads to the conclusion that 8–19% of the variation in student learning outcomes lies between schools with a further amount of up to 55% of the variation in individual learning outcomes between classrooms within schools.[2]

> Studies of school effectiveness and school improvement indicate that the classroom effect is greater than the whole school effect in explaining students' progress.[3]

> The influences on pupil achievement are multilevel and the net effect of classrooms was higher than that of schools.[4]

> All the evidence that has been generated in the school effectiveness research community shows that classrooms are far more important than schools in determining how children perform at school.[5]

So there is good reason for teachers to feel empowered about focusing on learning in their classrooms. Nevertheless, even with the balance of school and classroom put more appropriately, there is still reason for some attention to be given to the processes of the organisation which might promote or hinder the development of classrooms as learning communities.

Organisations that learn

We accept that individual humans learn. Previous chapters address how to help a group learn. Can an organisation learn? Entertain for a moment an image of an organisation, as:

> where people continually expand their capacity to create the results they truly desire, where new and expansive patterns of thinking are nurtured, where collective aspiration is set free, and where people are continually learning to see the whole together.[6]

This brief description of a learning organisation comes from a book which was identified by *Harvard Business Review* as one of the seminal management books of the past seventy-five years, which has sold more than a million copies, and which was written by someone who in business circles has been named a 'Strategist of the Century'. But the book is not about schools.

Its description of an organisation stands in contrast to the dominant model which circulates in most of our schools. The common unexamined 'mental model' is of a machine: a collection of interlocking parts, each playing a clearly separated function in the whole; run by routines, timetables and clocks; managed by organisation structure, hierarchy and specialised division of labour; 'line managers' who monitor work performance[7] and talk of 'efficiency, reliability, predictability and objectives'. And of course machines are deemed to run best when they run smoothly and at their own pace, thus defining the required behaviour and pace of the humans.

It's no surprise that politicians whose world is closely associated with bureaucracy should emphasise the mechanical view of organisations, but it is a cruel act that they should try to impose it on schools, and on the crucial aspect of humans which does not fit such a model – learning.

Indeed in many aspects of business and commerce – even a large number of factories – the approach to organisations has become one which much more attempts to harness and connect the capacities of its members, so that the organisation thinks ahead, pays attention to its context, seeks to embrace change, and solves problems by thinking widely throughout the organisation.[8]

Indeed, in many aspects of business and commerce – even a large number of factories – the approach to organisations has become one which much more attempts to harness and connect the capacities of its members, so that it becomes an organisation which thinks ahead, pays attention to its context, seeks to embrace change, and solves problems by thinking throughout the organisation.[9] The developing literature on organisational learning in schools reflects such themes.[10]

Schools as learning organisations

Schools are not commercial businesses, so they may have their own reasons for becoming more effective learning organisations. These can be identified at a number of levels:

- *For the pupils*: schools which are to promote pupils' effective learning for the future need to continually review how best this can be achieved in a fast-changing world. And as that world changes and we embrace learners from different cultures, our conception of learning can be enriched.[11]
- *For the staff*: one of the strongest imperatives for building a learning organisation is that we want to be in one. Teachers regularly report that the variety in their professional work is a value, and the school needs to support them in learning from that variety.
- *For the organisation*: the environment for schools is increasingly fast-changing, and schools' position in a 'marketised' situation is more unstable, so that they need to take on the characteristics of learning organisations to ensure a continued contribution.

Do any current schools function as learning organisations? The answer is 'Yes', but for a host of reasons not as many as one might expect or hope.[12] Studies of successful schools, in the UK and other countries, including those that are successful in the performance view of politicians, continue to provide evidence of the important features.

A recent study of secondary schools in South Australia[13] employed a survey of 2,000 teachers and principals. It identified four dimensions of schools as a learning organisations:

- *Trusting and collaborative climate* refers to a school where collaboration is the norm. Teachers participate in most significant school-level policy decisions and help to establish the school's vision or goals. Discussions among colleagues are open and candid and information is shared with other members of the school community including parents. Staff are valued.
- *Taking initiatives and risks* refers to staff being empowered to make decisions and feeling free to experiment and take risks. The school structures support teacher initiatives, the administrators promote enquiry and dialogue and are open to change.
- *Shared and monitored mission* refers to a school culture that encourages critical examination of current practices and continuous learning for improvement. The school staff keep abreast of external events that may impact on their school. The curriculum is aligned with the school's vision and goals. Information from other schools and from professional associations is used to support learning.
- *Professional development* refers to the engagement of staff in professional development. Professional reading is a source of learning and so are other schools. Developing skills of how to work and learn in teams is seen as important. External advice is sought as appropriate and school leaders provide all the support they can to promote professional development.

Successful schools focus on learning

It is a focus on learning which improves performance. A major study of UK secondary schools[14] identified schools in which pupils had improved their performance above the rate of national improvement in the 1990s. These schools have taken various approaches:

1   new tactics to maximise their showing in the performance tables (enter more pupils, mentor the borderlines, etc.);
2   internal strategies to improve their schools (giving more responsibility to pupils, building improvement strategies in particular departments, integrating pastoral and academic responsibilities);
3   the small group of the highest improving schools has shifted beyond these two into an area which builds its capacity to improve, through an overarching focus on learning.

Successful schools are not compliant

In a study of seventy-eight schools, Susan Rosenholtz[15] found evidence to divide her sample into 'moving schools' and 'stuck schools' on a range of indicators. Her survey of teachers included the question: 'Do you ever have to do things that are against the rules in order to do what's best for your students?'. In Moving schools 79 per cent answered 'Yes'. In Stuck schools 75 per cent answered 'No'.

Moving schools are also learning-enriched, in which teachers' find more opportunities to learn, and they see their own learning as cumulative and developmental. Students' gains are greater in reading and in maths, and this is significantly related to teachers' learning opportunities and the extent to which teachers see teaching as non-routine. So the connection is clear: '*We also find that the greater teachers' opportunities for learning, the more their students tend to learn*'.

Successful schools are collaborative

Moving schools have above-average teacher collaboration, there are more requests for and offers of collegial advice and these operate on a wider range than in low-collaboration schools. The content of discussions about learners is more productive, focusing on improving their learning rather than on seeking sympathy about poor behaviour.

Collaboration between teachers leads to them feeling collectively interested in the learning in the organisation, and this is reflected in better results for students.[16]

Successful schools focus on connections

A hallmark of learning is that it creates new connections – between meanings, experiences, contexts and people. So too for schools. A recent survey of UK primary schools, which had been selected as successful in performance terms, showed that their curriculum made connections across subjects, used themes for planning, did not overemphasise 'core' subjects, and provided many enriching experiences beyond the bounds of the school gates and the school day.[17] One of the keys to success that stood out for all schools was 'The pupils understand the nature and purpose of their learning, in some cases contributing to the planning and evaluation of the curriculum'.

With some of the above broad characteristics in place, I find that people often start to ask 'practical' questions about how a school operates as a learning organisation, what it looks like, and so on. Unfortunately, the way these questions are framed often betrays the way we have been socialised to view organisations: 'How often are the meetings?' 'What does the head do?' and the like. These questions seek a solution in routine and structure, and turn out to be the features of the old 'mental model' which actually make the journey towards becoming a learning organisation more of an 'against the current' experience than might be expected.[18] A learning organisation does not work with fixed formulae for achieving its goals, or a fixed structure: it has both goals and structure, but more important than either of these is the fact that it reviews both of these, and asks of each of its activities 'what did we learn as a result of this?'. In this way the core culture of learning is built: there is a commitment to learning, talk about learning, and reviews of the way that the organisation views itself and what impedes learning.[19]

But is this yet the school as a learning community? Without over-polarising, the following contrast may further our thinking. *In a learning organisation*, the ends of importance are organisational growth, productivity, efficiency and effectiveness. The means are the people and the learning they do in support of organisational goals. *In a learning community*, the ends of importance are the growth and development of the people. The means are the ways in which community members work and learn together.[20] Such a shift to learning community may remind us of the human goals of school and help release us from the model of the machine.

Schools as learning communities

In Chapter 4, evidence on the effects of operating schools as communities was reviewed, to provide context for the review of the effects of operating classrooms this way. When students feel a sense of community and staff build cohesion, the social relations build the connection to school and to achievement. Pupils are more highly motivated and engaged in learning and more committed to school when they experience acceptance, and a sense of belonging. Engagement and commitment are closely linked to student performance, and, more importantly, to the quality of student learning.[21] 'Collective teacher efficacy is a significant predictor of student achievement'.[22]

Schools which operate as communities 'attend to the needs of students for affiliation and . . . provide a rich spectrum of adult roles. Adults engage students personally and challenge them to engage in the life of the school'.[23] School communities believe in a common core curriculum for all and that all pupils can achieve. There are collegial relations among adults coupled with a 'diffuse' teacher role (which brings them into frequent contact with other staff and with students in settings other than the classroom).

More recently it has been shown that such schools develop better trusting relations between staff, and that this relates not only to the levels of attainment of pupils, but also to the school's longer-term pattern of improvement.[24]

So how do schools operate as learning communities? At the heart must be the same hallmarks and processes which were identified in Chapter 3: agency, belonging, cohesion, diversity, plus enquiry, knowledge-generation and collective reflection. If these have been developing in classrooms, there will already be implications for the school community. When classrooms cease to operate as hermetically sealed delivery boxes, but as learning communities which go beyond the bounds, then some of the core processes will be starting to operate. When learning becomes a key focus of enquiry and public presence in classrooms, it is also likely to do so in the school at large, When better understanding of learning emerges in classrooms, they must be able to make the local decisions to promote it,[25] and so on.

When thinking of schools and school improvement, it is common to think of the 'leadership' and the teachers first. This risks reverting to the hierarchical model, so first I will outline some more of what is known about schools as learning communities in their widest sense: their relationships, values and culture. Some voices choose to call these the 'soft' aspect of organisations, and they may be correct in that they are not parts of a machine, but they are very wrong to suggest that these are nebulous or difficult to address. Some tough principles may emerge, and the challenge will then be for the leadership and the teachers to bring them to life.

Before addressing these areas, what experiences do you bring? What experiences have you had of schools which operate as a learning community? They may not be complete or commonplace experiences, but they do raise important pointers. The answers may sometimes seem paradoxical, as with one teacher who answered by telling me about a school which was closing, and in the years while numbers reduced, staff had to take on more connected tasks, a focus on the future was more developed, and so on. But whatever the examples, they may serve to link your voice to some of the principles (which have also been considered in classrooms):

- Acting collaboratively and fostering interdependence.
- Learning and reflecting as teams and other collectives.
- Distributed leadership.
- Public focus on learning.
- Looking beyond the bounds including to other communities of learning teachers.
- Scanning the environment.

School relationships matter

It is easy to recognise that the relationships in any organisation are key to its functioning, but not always so easy to talk about them. The language of relationships will need support as we leave behind the machine. One writer proposes, 'If we are going to be serious about community building, we are going to have to cross this language barrier by speaking more directly and humanly about schooling', and challenges us to ask whether we are into authentic community or counterfeit community.[26] Table 10.1 is developed from his view of how relationships differ in such different contexts.

Table 10.1 Relationships in authentic community and counterfeit community (after Sergiovanni 1994)

Affective Teachers' relationships with students are quite warm and engaging	*Affective neutrality* Teachers' relationships with students are like those of professional to client
Collective orientation Teachers encourage collaborative learning and support between students	*Self-orientation* Teachers encourage an individual orientation on the part of students
Particularism Teachers take into account the unique features of a disciplinary incident	*Universalism* Discipline incidents are dealt with according to predetermined protocols
Ascription Teachers value students for being whoever they are, regardless of how well they do	*Achievement* Teachers value students for their cooperation and achievement
Diffuseness Teachers believe 'You need to know students well to teach them well'	*Specificity* Teachers believe that they can enact their roles well with little tailoring to individuals
Substantive Teachers demonstrate care for students as a core value	*Instrumental* Teachers demonstrate care for students in order to get better results

The differences in Table 10.1 ring true to some of my experience of schools, including in the field of behaviour which causes concern. Those schools which, perhaps encouraged by government voices of the last decade, adopt predetermined protocols for responding to incidents often have higher levels of difficulty, exclusion, and so on. In more worrying behaviour, such as violence, our study of six inner-city secondary schools in areas of significant neighbourhood violence found:

It was very evident from our research that school practices do make a clear difference in the extent to which a school is resilient to its own situated potential for the occurrence of violence. Of particular significance are:

- The quality of relationships within schools – between staff and between staff and students.
- The quality and extent of communications within schools – including, especially, staff–student communications over violent incidents.
- The range of policies and practices for dealing with violence and its potential emergence.
- The engagement with and relationship to the neighbourhood of the school and its communities of interest.[27]

The schools with least violence were connected and communicative, internally and externally.

The school's values as a community matter

Some of the literature about schools as learning communities can seem vague. Much talk of 'sharing a vision' and 'sharing leadership' can miss the point if it inadvertently obscures the fact that the beliefs and values which are 'shared' make a crucial difference.

Close examination suggests that significant differences in beliefs and practices can exist in two schools which seemed to be two learning communities.[28] Whereas one school's community emphasises individual autonomy, rights and responsibilities to each, the other's emphasise a collective view of learning and schooling. Table 10.2 identifies some of the differences between these two schools.

Table 10.2 Differences in belief and practices in two schools

School A	School B
Shared beliefs in the purpose of schooling:	
To educate citizens who will obey constituted authority and respect the rights and property of others	To educate citizens who will be informed and participating members in a democratic society
To promote self-esteem for all students	To promote respect and dignity for all students
To have each student learn at his or her maximum level	To critically examine local and global social issues

in teaching strategies and curriculum:

Teachers meet and discuss individual classroom teaching practices and strategies	Teachers meet and discuss shared educational principles and collective practices and strategies
Individualised curriculum; varies by teacher's choice	Collectivised curriculum; interdisciplinary, project-based

Participation

Institutional policies allow participation	Institutional structures demand participation
Teachers attend meetings and staff development days	Teachers plan meetings and staff development days
Managers make decisions without input from teachers	Teachers make decisions and set school policies
Professional and personal commitments are often in conflict	Professional work engages personal and social commitments
New teachers seek autonomy and enforce boundaries between personal and professional life	New teachers drawn into climate of participation and blur personal and professional boundaries

Interdependence

Teachers support one another's individual classroom work and occasionally team-teach	Teachers intertwine classroom work through collective curriculum design and implementation
Primary curricular goals are subject-area defined (and therefore limited to subject-area teachers)	Primary curricular goals are interdisciplinary, defined by ideals of social justice and participation

Dissent

Broad, generalised beliefs allow many objectives to coexist; participation in public forums is limited and selective	Openly specified beliefs result in self-selection; some teachers leave; among those who remain, participation is widespread and extensive
Dissent is rarely voiced in public forums	Dissent is voiced in public legitimated spaces

Relationships

Teachers care for one another; professional and personal commitments are often in conflict	Professional and personal relationships are intertwined; work engages both personal and social commitments

The content of Table 10.2 shows how markedly schools which seem to be communities might differ, and differ along lines which were identified over a century ago (see Tönnies, Chapter 3).

A learning culture

'Culture' is a term used in thinking about organisations, which can sometimes have a mystifying effect. Interpreting culture as 'the way we do things around here' has never been particularly illuminating for me. However, the narrative stance[29] which proposes that 'culture is the ensemble of stories we tell ourselves about ourselves' is very applicable to organisations, and also enables a more achievable approach to culture change.

An account from a London primary school was provided by Jess, who was at that time Deputy Head. A range of events had led to Learning about Learning being made part of the School Improvement Plan. Staff meetings, usually one or two each term, and half-termly professional dialogue and review meetings were held where ideas on learning were often reviewed. Over two years Jess felt that the culture had noticeably changed. Jess lists her analysis of the change as follows:

Factors in helping shift the culture

- Learning about learning was planned as a focus, it was built in and there to stay in the School Improvement Plan.
- Having staff on-side made a difference – they were willing to join in discussions and experiment with ideas in their classrooms.
- Staff were invited to try things. The opportunity to develop their own practice in their own way was invitational and some staff found this empowering.
- Time was given to reflect and discuss practice, to share successes and try each others' ideas out and to try and help with any difficulties.

Successes

- Time to talk about learning and develop our practice is now accepted as what we do in our school.
- New staff have strengthened the culture and have accepted positively what they have walked into.
- Staff and children are more able to talk about learning with some understanding and a shared language and therefore more able to sustain a debate about how children learn.
- Teachers are willing to try things and experiment and to come up with their own ideas and implement them in their classrooms.
- There is a collective and shared belief that we need to keep talking about learning and work against the grain.
- My role during meetings has shifted to being more a facilitator rather than a leader.
- Teachers are more aware of the different aspects of learning, e.g. concepts of learning, orientations and styles of learning, motivation and self-esteem.
- Little changes have taken place with BIG meanings.

Issues

- Initially, meetings were seen by some staff as a luxury. They felt that there were more important things to do with their time.
- It is hard working against the grain; trying to shift thinking in a performance-oriented wider context – tests, SATs etc. – to one that is more learning-oriented within our school context. We were always sensing the push and pull in our discussions and in what we felt we were being expected to do in our practice.
- New staff were inducted via specific meetings and introduced to the main ideas which the old staff had already looked at. This helped with their assimilation into future staff meetings.
- We are still developing a shared language when talking about learning. Staff find it easier to talk about themselves as learners but harder to bring that into the classroom.

For me, the points about language are strong here, and relate to the promotion of experiment and review as well as what can make such a development difficult. These are the very elements which provide a key focus for development, through the best route possible – learning. The sort of culture which can emerge in a school would be somehow similar to that I witnessed in Robin Hood school, where, at morning break, the staff were talking about learners and learning over their morning coffee. When teachers learn more about learning, the effectiveness of a school improves and increased performance follows, especially for many of the under-achieving students.[30]

Jess's account was not focused on ways in which pupils and others were involved. This is a clear feature at a school nearby where Kathryn is the head learner. She describes her 'Super learners in the early years!', and a learning journey for a small-maintained nursery school which has led to a variety of exploratory action research involving children, families, governors and staff.

I first started to look at learning from the adult perspectives of my colleagues whom I asked to describe in a staff meeting when they felt they learnt best. Comments included:

1   'I learn best through a new experience.'
2   'Making mistakes – some bad experiences give you the greatest experience of learning, e.g. giving birth, divorce, family deaths.
3   'A hands-on experience.'

Next I asked parents for their views and perspectives about what they felt they wanted their child to learn by the time they leave us and go into the Reception class. The results included three types:

1   'To develop a better understanding of numbers, to recognise some letters of the alphabet.' Or 'To sit down for 25–30 minutes and focus on one particular point.'

2   'To share toys and be fair with peers.' Or 'To develop their social and emotional skills to enable them to mix socially with other children and make friends.'

3   'To have a general liking to learn new things.' Or 'My ideal would be for him to begin to learn that love of knowledge – all knowledge – and to know that he will be rewarded for an inquisitive mind. Also for him to have the confidence to ask questions and experiment for himself. These attributes would set him up for the rest of his life and would mean he could learn most things for himself.'

This helped me understand that my next obvious learning challenge was to gain the children's viewpoint about learning. Thus I set up a videoed discussion with two groups of 3- and 4-year-old children as to 'What is learning?'. A range of views included:

1   'You have to learn to talk and say things when you are a baby. You learn when you're with different people by listening and trying to talk. Babies have to practise.'

2   'Playing outside is different learning – you learn by watching then having a go.'

Our learning focus has also led, I believe, to us becoming more unconsciously inclusive in whom we see as part of our professional learning community. My evidence for this is through our two most recent parents' evenings where we have provided more interactive learning workshops where parents and governors join in staff-led activities about aspects of the children's learning. The first workshop was about aspects of creative role-play and designing/making resources based around transport in London. The second parent's evening was based around learning through challenge, problem-solving, collaboration and cooperation.

Finally, as our oldest children prepare to leave us and move to Reception classes I asked them to represent what learning is through drawing.

> These are the starting stages of a whole school learning journey,
> which has allowed us to start to wrestle with learning, its owner-
> ship, and the boundaries and power-sharing/struggles which are
> linked to learning in schools in a society which sees learning as a
> buzzword for the future development of the world.

Teachers' professional community

As we turn our focus back towards teachers, it is now appropriate to ask
how a learning community between teachers is to be promoted in a
school. For a number of years it has been shown that the characteristics
of teachers' professional community in schools include:

- A collective focus on student learning.
- Reflective dialogue.
- Collaboration to move beyond the bounds of the box classroom.

Thinking about how to develop this in everyday schools has highlighted:

- Structural conditions: time to meet, interdependence, and so on.
- Social and human resources: trust and respect.

Structural responses are a common focus but are only part of the
answer. A common mechanism is that of creating teacher teams, which
does have a positive impact on teacher empowerment and teacher
collaboration, but it does not necessarily lead to a greater focus on
learning. In one study 'Teams reported spending about 25% of their
time on administrative work, 30% on student discipline issues, 20% on
paperwork from their school and district, and the remaining time on
teaching and learning issues'.[31] Team structures provide a foundation,
but do not on their own influence the culture of learning and teaching.
One of the reasons suggested for this is that teachers do not have the
experience and models for how to do it. So the old mechanistic view of
organisations come to fill their meetings, rather than a focus on learning.
Nevertheless, in the minority of schools where such a shift does occur,
student performance improves, and is related to three attributes:

1   teacher teams prepare collaboratively, and discuss student learning in relation to teaching approaches;
2   teachers sometimes teach together, observe each other teaching, and feel safe doing so;
3   teacher teams handle pupil groupings flexibly and purposefully, regrouping students to take advantage of the strengths of team members and of small groups for particular purposes.

Team learning has also been a focus of study. There is significant variation in the nature and amount of learning across teams in secondary schools. For most enriched learning a culture which supports and demonstrates respect for teachers' agency, collaboration and diversity is required. 'For the team's thinking to be constructive, the leader needs to encourage diversity of viewpoints and an atmosphere of open inquiry.'[32]

Overall, the view emerging is that 'Our research suggests that human resources – such as openness to improvement, trust and respect, teachers having knowledge and skills, supportive leadership and socialization – are more critical to the development of professional community than structural conditions.'[33]

Evidence to support this approach to development is supportive, including for its contribution to pupil attainment. A study on 11,000 students enrolled in 820 US secondary schools identified the extent to which the schools were characterised by professional learning communities. In those which were most characterised this way, the staff had worked together and changed their classroom pedagogy. As a result, they engaged students in high intellectual learning tasks, and students achieved greater academic gains in maths, science, history and reading than students in traditionally organised schools. In addition, the achievement gaps between students from different backgrounds were smaller in these schools, students learned more, and, in the smaller high schools, learning was distributed more equitably.[34] Other researchers have found higher levels of professional community to be associated with higher student achievement, though again, associations between classroom practices and achievement are stronger.[35] Most recently, analyses of a national sample of US secondary schools confirms the findings from in-depth studies and studies of purposeful samples that the social organisation of teachers and schools can affect student achievement.[36]

Here a connection has been made between professional community and the style of headteacher leadership, noting a positive effect on the measured student attainments in schools whose teachers experience above-average transformational leadership.

In US primary schools too, data from 5,690 teachers in 248 schools in a large urban school district shows the impact of structural, human and social factors on the emergence of school-based professional community and examines the extent to which such developments in turn promote learning and experimentation among staff.[37] By far, the strongest facilitator of professional community is social trust among faculty members. Principal leadership and supervision that was facilitative emerged as important facilitating variables. Principals' regular involvement goes beyond regular contact, and encourages teachers to be involved, to innovate and to take risks. In general, an environment that supports innovation and experimentation was found to be much more prevalent in schools in which professional community had developed. Results lead to the view that if professional community in fact fosters classroom change, it does so by creating an environment that supports teacher learning through innovation and experimentation.

Leadership

Being appointed as the formal leader of a school organisation attracts many dynamics to make the role ineffective. Some people will display infantile paralysis and 'wait for orders', while others will ask a head to deal with everything, most important the toilets. Such processes of 'role-sending' reflect an unstated assumption about leaders – they are powerful people – yet their impact achieves the opposite. Evidence on leadership over decades contradicts the 'leaders are born' mentality. Leadership is not boss-ship, as you might be forgiven for thinking from such phenomena as leadership programmes.

Leaders display a range of complexities. 'If they ain't following, you ain't leading' is the phrase which reminds us that this role like all others can only be understood in terms of relationships. My use of the term 'formal leader' is also intended to indicate another complexity, that there are any number of informal leaders in a school, as in a classroom. So the formally appointed leader has to develop a multiple web of relationships, and there is no one way to behave.

The most effective stance for understanding leadership is one which relates quickly to the leading of learning communities. It thinks of leadership as distributed throughout an organisation, just as knowledge may be seen in this way. So 'Leadership practice is distributed over leaders, followers, and the school's situation or context'.[38] A study of ninety-six secondary schools concluded that the key elements in student outcomes are participation and engagement.[39] Successful leadership in these schools stressed support, care, trust and participation: this contrasts with current government rhetoric of leaders having 'drive', acting decisively, giving clear direction and having impact by persuasion. Another study examined twenty schools and identified those which were more 'ready' to become professional learning communities. In these schools, principals sometimes elicited staff dreams and visions for the school, and 'those who co-created or presented an agreed-upon vision seemed to have buy-in'. Visions moved beyond test-scores. Principals empowered others to make decisions, and responsibilities were dispersed.[40]

Leaders in every part of a school which operates as a learning community will need to support the processes of review and reflection, finding their own best way to discuss and learn about whether practice is achieving the vision. But research into organisational learning has identified that this loop of learning needs to be accompanied by another: the review of whether the vision is appropriate.[41] A study of three schools suggested that this 'double loop learning invaluable to sustain professional community'.[42]

'Leading learning' is a phrase which is beginning to be heard more. It can mean many different things, depending on the view of leadership and the view of learning. In line with other elements of this book, I offer a view that distinguishes what different leaders might do dependent on which of the three views of learning they adopt:[43]

---

1   '*Learning = being taught*'. Leaders who see learning from this perspective are likely to:
    •   focus on teachers more than learners, especially their knowledge and 'competences';

- view the process of curriculum as one of delivering a body of knowledge;
- value tangible products which are deemed to be easily measurable;
- favour modes of assessment which are timed, summative performance tests, often through paper-and-pencil methods;
- seek to improve performance by accelerating the pace at which learners get 'it' into their heads;
- drive improvement through measurable indicators of product;
- talk about learning in ways that conflate learning with teaching and performance;
- de-emphasise the social dimensions and social outcomes of learning.

2   '*Learning = individual sense-making*'. Leaders who see learning from this perspective are likely to:
- focus on the way people make sense of their experiences;
- view curriculum as addressing thought-demanding questions;
- value processes which make learning a visible, central element: making reasoning public, thinking aloud together;
- favour modes of assessment which ask people to explain to one another, give a reflective commentary;
- seek to improve learning by slowing down the pace and focusing on quality of thinking;
- drive improvement through indicators of quality learning experiences;
- talk publicly about learning, and promote enquiry into learning;
- support learning exchanges and peer teaching;
- promote people known as learners;

- ask of every policy and every procedure: 'What do we learn from this?';
- encourage others to do the above.

3 '*Learning = building knowledge as part of doing things with others*'. Leaders who see learning from this perspective are likely to:
- focus on social and collaborative processes in teams and classes;
- view curriculum as a process of building and testing knowledge;
- view learning as a process of action and dialogue which leads to improvement in knowledge;
- value processes which enhance collaborative and community outcomes;
- favour modes of assessment which provide a community product;
- seek to improve learning by enhancing collaborative enquiry and dialogue;
- orchestrate improvement through indicators of the learning culture;
- talk about learning as a distributed process of building knowledge, so that all can be involved;[44]
- talk about leadership as a distributed process of building culture, so that all can be involved;
- ensure fluid organisation, spanning boundaries.

Being learning-enriched in current times

My experience is that many classroom teachers and many teachers in formal leadership roles have a preferred vision of classrooms and schools which bears similarity with that of this book. But as this chapter suggests, they cite the current times as reason for their practices which work against the vision. There is no need for our profession to go backwards just because politicians do, but saying that highlights one of the extra elements in the repertoire of teachers which is needed in current times, and has not been so much needed heretofore. It is being able to maintain vision, and maintain faith, while having to act strategically in relation to the forces which circulate in the wider environment. Yes, schools need to have data on the achievements of their pupils: in some cases it leads to them being able to demonstrate to the agents of prescriptive practice that their way does not work. Yes, schools have to go through hostile inspections, and some schools have learned a lot about how not to be damaged by this process – they are often very learning-oriented schools and although the inspection framework is poor at identifying this, a reasonable inspection team will be able to indicate it in the report. One primary school has the word 'learning' mentioned twenty-three times in its report, and from my knowledge of that school it is an appropriate reflection. By contrast, a search of the Ofsted inspection database shows that the phrase 'learning communities' seldom arises, and many of its occurrences are merely a synonym for school.

How do schools maintain themselves to be learning-enriched in such times? By operating in all the ways highlighted in this chapter: collaborative, distributed and resolutely focused on learning. Plus having a thought-out 'big picture' of what is happening to schools, and a vision to contribute in that context. The ones I know are modest yet inspiring places. In that big picture they have an awareness of the forces that act against them.

Managing the forces against change

At times in each chapter I have attempted to identify the processes through which external pressures become internalised and appear in teachers' practice. The understanding of how we hear and respond to a range of voices has helped me to resist this process and continue a contribution. What also helps is the opportunity to talk about the process with others. Most of the teachers I meet are able to resist the many invitations to compliance, and they call on very important resources in their family, cultural and community life. And I am sure that the act of identifying and naming the voices which undermine our vision is effective in decreasing their life-negating impact. Analysing how those voices operate is a major step in undoing their impact.

Some commentators have a critical analysis of the current times, but a less hopeful stance in the development of learning communities. They may summarise 'whilst it may be possible to conceptualise the leadership of a learning community, it may nevertheless be impossible to realise it because of a failure to see and counter an ecology of the forces which surrounds leadership and learning communities'.[45] I believe this stance stems from overstating the power of ecological forces, and understating the human propensity to define oneself locally.

The local forces are important, and often highlight the tensions of teaching. As we take steps to resolve those tensions in a new way, a degree of risk may be felt. The biggest risk in education is not to take one, so we must beware the tendency to step back into the dominant patterns. Marlene Scardamalia writes about educators who visit a knowledge-building classroom, and the barriers to adoption they may create:

> The first, and most insidious – because it seldom comes out in the open – is the disbelief that most children have the motivation and ability to do the things the educator has just witnessed. This shows up first as a suggestion that the children and the teacher, or both, are exceptional. In practice it shows up as a tendency to over-structure and over-manage activity, with the result that some of the essential characteristics of knowledge building are sacrificed.[46]

The challenge which is embedded in this book is only the challenge of being a teacher, which is to create a proactive culture in the classroom. It will not reflect some aspects of the surrounding culture but will act as a model of what that surrounding culture might become, and is becoming, in some quarters.

Prompts for reflection

- Think about schools you have known, and schools you can imagine. How does the school as an organisation show recognition that the classroom is the key site for learning?

- There are many elements which can contribute to the building of learning communities. Which aspects are most needed in your school?
- In a community, leadership is distributed, and this situation emerges through more people taking on leadership roles. In what ways might you be able to lead an improvement in the learning culture of your school?

A concluding remark

If you are a reader who likes to turn to the end of a book first, in order to find out 'who done it' my main contender for the villain of the piece is our language. My hope is that this book will help to shift the conversations.

Notes

Chapter 1

1 Wrigley (2000).
2 OECD (2001a).
3 *Times Educational Supplement*, 12 January 2001, p. 61.

Chapter 2

1 The positioning of letter keys on your keyboard was defined by the metal
   hammers of a typewriter and minimising the number of occasions when
   adjacent letters locked together while striking the paper. Still relevant for
   the majority of word processor keyboards. See Waldrop (1994) for further
   discussion of 'lock-in'.
2 Cuban (1993a, 1993b); Sarason (1993).
3 Broadfoot (1987, p. 31).
4 Sarason (1993, pp. 7, 33 and 91).
5 Marble *et al.* (2000).
6 Deci *et al.* (1982); Deci and Ryan (1982).
7 Stodolsky and Grossman (2000).
8 Sfard (1998).
9 Sullivan (2000).
10 Doyle (1990).
11 Developed from Watkins *et al.* (2002).
12 Corrie *et al.* (1982).

Chapter 3

1 Harvey-Jones (1995).
2 Sergiovanni (1994, p. 3).
3 Tönnies (1887 [1957]).
4 Johnson, S.M. (1990).
5 Watkins, C. (2003a).

6   Schlechty (1990).
7   Watkins, P. (1996).
8   Gromyko and Maurice (2000).
9   Rutter *et al.* (1979).
10 Bryk and Driscoll (1988); Bryk *et al.* (1990, 1993).
11 Bayliss (1999).
12 Gergen (1991, p. 3, then p. 61).
13 Dietz and Burns (1992).
14 Bandura (2000).
15 Goodenow (1992); Goodenow and Grady (1993).
16 Fiol (1996).
17 Shields (1999).
18 Dewey (1916).
19 Hannikainen and van Oers (1999).
20 Axelrod (1990).
21 Johnson *et al.* (1994).
22 Galton and Williamson (1992).
23 Johnson, B. (2003).
24 Especially Brown and Campione (1996).
25 Wells (1999, 2000).
26 Brown and Campione (1994); Palincsar *et al.* (1998); Scardamalia *et al.* (1994).
27 Latour and Woolgar (1992).
28 Orr (1997).
29 As Schwartz and Lin (2001) point out, Marx (1939 [1973]) spoke of these as the two great forces that constitute a person.
30 Freire (1970).
31 Perkins (1994).
32 Wells (2002a).
33 Bereiter (2002a); Wells (2002b).
34 Blair (1998, p. 12).
35 Solomon, Schaps *et al.* (1992).
36 Davis (2003).
37 Atkinson (1999).
38 I have encountered different views on whether John Flavell or Ann Brown coined the term. See, for example, Flavell (1976) and Brown (1975).
39 Watkins *et al.* (1998) or Watkins *et al.* (2000).
40 Watkins, C. (2001).
41 Bryson and Scardamalia (1996).
42 Powell and Makin (1994).

Chapter 4

1   Wang *et al.* (1990).
2   Marzano (1998).
3   Watkins (2003b).

4 Driver *et al.* (1994).
5 Cobb and Bauersfeld (1995).
6 Peterson *et al.* (1989).
7 Staub and Stern (2002).
8 Inagaki *et al.* (1998).
9 Abbott and Fouts (2003).
10 Scardamalia and Bereiter (1994).
11 Prawat and Peterson (1999).
12 Bryk and Driscoll (1988).
13 Lee and Smith (1995).
14 Lewis *et al.* (1996).
15 Goodenow (1992).
16 Goodenow and Grady (1993).
17 Hagborg (1998).
18 Israelashvili (1997).
19 Roeser *et al.* (1996).
20 Voelkl (1997).
21 Battistich and Hom (1997).
22 Schaps and Solomon (2003).
23 Resnick *et al.* (1993).
24 Resnick *et al.* (1997).
25 OECD (2001b).
26 Willms (2003).
27 Osterman (1998).
28 Battistich *et al.* (1996).
29 Battistich *et al.* (1997).
30 Schaps (2003).
31 Battistich *et al.* (1999).
32 Dietz and Burns (1992).
33 Schwartz and Lin (2001).
34 Scardamalia and Bereiter (1991).
35 Bandura (2000).
36 Leithwood and Jantzi (2000).
37 Connell and Wellborn (1991).
38 Johnson *et al.* (1995).
39 Battistich *et al.* (1995).
40 Deci *et al.* (1991).
41 Ryan (1995).
42 Battistich (2001).
43 Connell *et al.* (1995).
44 Solomon *et al.* (1996).
45 Benninga *et al.* (1991).
46 Schaps and Solomon (1990).
47 Solomon *et al.* (1997).
48 Battistich *et al.* (1994).
49 Schaps *et al.* (1997).

50 Elbers and Streefland (2000a).
51 Rafal (1996).
52 Christal *et al.* (1997).
53 Williams and Downing (1998).
54 Elbers (2003).
55 Solomon, Watson *et al.* (1992).
56 Scardamalia and Bereiter (1992).
57 Hakkarainen and Sintonen (2002).
58 Hakkarainen (1995).
59 Elbers (2003).
60 Engle and Conant (2002).
61 Brown *et al.* (1993).
62 Elbers and Streefland (2000b).
63 Osterman (1998).
64 Cohen (1995).
65 Cohen and Scardamalia (1998).
66 Crawford *et al.* (1999).
67 Schwartz (1995).
68 Anderman and Anderman (1999).
69 Palincsar and Brown (1984).
70 Brown and Campione (1994).
71 Brown (1997).
72 Campione *et al.* (1995).
73 Schaps and Lewis (1999).
74 Paavola *et al.* (2002).
75 Scardamalia and Bereiter (1996).
76 Bereiter *et al.* (1997).
77 Scardamalia (2002).
78 Ryser *et al.* (1995).
79 Lamon *et al.* (1993).
80 Lamon *et al.* (2001).
81 Caswell and Bielaczyc (2002).
82 Mason (1998).
83 Hogan (2001).
84 Hakkarainen (2003).
85 Hume (2000).
86 Lipponen (2002).
87 Miyake and Koschmann (2002).
88 Bielaczyc (2001).
89 Bereiter (2002b).
90 Forman and Ansell (2001).
91 Dawes *et al.* (2000); Mercer (2002); Wegerif and Dawes (2004).

Interlude

1 See Watkins and Whalley (1993).
2 Watkins (1998, 2000a).

Chapter 5

1 See McNeil (2000) for an account of how standardised testing leads to a 'noncurriculum' which discriminates against minorities, and makes access to knowledge less communal and more stratified.
2 Dictionary definition of an accountant: 'One that keeps, audits and inspects the financial records of individuals or business concerns and prepares reports' (Houghton Mifflin Dictionary 2000). Note the similarity with the style of inspection which has been introduced into education.
3 See Deci and Ryan (1982) and Deci *et al.* (1982).
4 Sarason (1993, p. 82).
5 Independent Radio News, 2 February 2001.
6 Chris Woodhead, *Daily Telegraph* (5 March 2001).
7 Office for Standards in Education (2002).
8 Featherstone *et al.* (1997).
9 For a teacher's analysis of 'delivery' and 'ventriloquy' in his current experience, see Sullivan (2000).
10 Positioning theory examines everyday language and discourse and how it constructs the local moral order, the shifting patterns of intentions, speaking and acting within which different groups become differently positioned. See Harré and Langenhove (1999).
11 Clarke *et al.* (2001).
12 See Paradise (1998).
13 Ryan and Deci (2000, p. 57).
14 Deci *et al.* (1999).
15 Ryan and Deci (2000).
16 From Nicholls and Thorkildsen (1995).
17 Deci *et al.* (1991).
18 Paris and Paris (2001); Boekaerts (1999); Areglado *et al.* (1997).
19 Starnes and Paris (2000, p. 397).
20 Sharan and Sharan (1992).
21 Nicholls and Thorkildsen (1995).
22 Atkinson (1999).
23 Donoahue (2003).
24 Boekaerts (2002, p. 601).
25 Dweck (1991); Markus and Kitayama (1991).
26 Kitayama *et al.* (1997).
27 Markus and Kitayama (1994).
28 Eckert *et al.* (1996).

Chapter 6

1 Doyle (1990); see also Doyle (1983, 1984, 1986) and Watkins and Wagner (2000).
2 Russell (1930).
3 Especially the 1988 Education Act, Section 4, paragraph 3: 'An order made under subsection (2) above may not require – (a) that any particular period or periods of time should be allocated during any key stage to the teaching of any programme of study or any matter, skill or process forming part of it; or (b) that provision of any particular kind should be made in school timetables for the periods to be allocated to such teaching during any stage'.
4 See Bloome *et al.* (1989).
5 Hughes (1997).
6 Brooks and Brooks (1999).
7 Bartsch and Wellman (1995).
8 Anderson *et al.* (1985).
9 Gibbs (1988).
10 Dennison and Kirk (1990), drawing on Kolb (1984).
11 Meece and Miller (1999).
12 Miller and Meece (1999).
13 Clifford (1990).
14 Clifford (1988).
15 Watkins (2001).
16 Turner (1995).
17 Perry (1998).
18 Hall *et al.* (1999).
19 Brown and Campione (1996).
20 Labaree (1997).
21 Gokhale (1995).
22 Lamon *et al.* (2001).
23 Hume (2000).
24 Short and Burke (1991); Short (1990); Heald-Taylor (1996).
25 Jalongo (1991, pp. 29, 30).
26 Alfie Kohn (2002) keynote address to American Association of Colleges for Teacher Education, New York; download from www.alfiekohn.org.
27 Bayliss (1999); Bayliss and others (2002); RSA (2003).
28 International Baccalaureate Organisation (2001, p. 23).

Chapter 7

1 Wang *et al.* (1990).
2 Scardamalia (2002).
3 Caswell and Bielaczyc (2002).
4 Lamon *et al.* (2001).
5 Attributed to Harry S. Truman; exact source unknown.

6 Yvonne Kurz (2003) Report for MA in Effective Learning, University of London Institute of Education.
7 Lou *et al.* (1996).
8 Mercer (2002).
9 Levine (2003, p. 28).
10 Wegerif and Mercer (1997); Dixon (1998).
11 van Zee and Minstrell (1997a, 1997b).
12 Palincsar and Brown (1984).
13 Rosenshine and Meister (1994).
14 Brown and Campione (1998).
15 Moore and Scevak (1995).
16 Aronson *et al.* (1977); Aronson and Bridgeman (1979).
17 Aronson and Patnoe (1997).
18 Knight and Bohlmeyer (1990).
19 Slavin (1987).
20 Steinbrink *et al.* (1995).
21 Holliday (2002).
22 Brown and Campione (1994).

Chapter 8

1 Bielaczyc and Collins (2000).
2 Cuban (1993a).
3 Hewitt and Scardamalia (1996).
4 Scardamalia (2003).
5 From Knowledge Forum site at http://www.knowledgeforum.com/K-12/inAction.htm.
6 Van Tassell (2000). See also Donoahue *et al.* (1996).
7 Hume (2000).
8 Haneda and Wells (2000).
9 Caswell and Lamon (1999).
10 Scardamalia *et al.* (1994).
11 Donoahue (2003).
12 Scardamalia and Bereiter (1999).

Chapter 9

1 Watkins and Wagner (2000).
2 Watkins, C. (2000a).
3 Kohn (1996).
4 Weimer (2002).
5 Short (1990).
6 Donoahue (2003).
7 Prawat (1992).

Interlude

1 Wrigley (2000).
2 Little (1988).
3 Watkins (2000b).
4 Abbreviated from Ofsted (2003).
5 Abbreviated from 'Teaching Attributes Observation Protocol', Brown and Fouts (2003).
6 Thomas (2003).

Chapter 10

1 Hill (1998, p. 423).
2 Cuttance (1998, p. 1158).
3 Stoll (1999, p. 504).
4 Kyriakides *et al.* (2000, p. 501).
5 Muijs and Reynolds (2001, p. vii).
6 Senge (1990, p. 3).
7 Morgan (1988).
8 Watkins (2004a).
9 Watkins and Marsick (1993, 1996); Bohl (1994).
10 Leithwood and Louis (1998).
11 Watkins, D. (2000).
12 Gray (2000).
13 Silins *et al.* (2002).
14 Gray *et al.* (1999).
15 Rosenholtz (1991).
16 Lee and Smith (1996).
17 Ofsted (2002).
18 Rait (1995).
19 Stoll *et al.* (2004).
20 Mitchell and Sackney (2000).
21 Osterman (2000).
22 Goddard *et al.* (2000).
23 Bryk and Driscoll (1988).
24 Bryk and Schneider (2002).
25 Supovitz (2002).
26 Developed from Sergiovanni (1994).
27 Hewitt *et al.* (2003). See also Watkins *et al.* (2005).
28 Westheimer (1999) based on Westheimer (1998).
29 See Wagner and Watkins (2005).
30 Munro (1999).
31 Supovitz (2002).
32 Leithwood *et al.* (1997, p. 319).
33 Kruse *et al.* (1994); see also Kruse *et al.* (1995).
34 Lee *et al.* (1995).

35 Louis and Marks (1998).
36 Wiley (2001).
37 Bryk *et al.* (1999).
38 Spillane *et al.* (2004).
39 Mulford and Silins (2003).
40 Hipp and Huffman (2000).
41 Reed and Stoll (2000).
42 Scribner *et al.* (1999).
43 Watkins (2004b).
44 Brown *et al.* (1993).
45 Bottery (2003).
46 Scardamalia (2002).

References

Abbott, M.L. and Fouts, J.T. (2003) *Constructivist Teaching and Student Achievement: the results of a school-level classroom observation study in Washington*, Lynnwood, WA: Seattle Pacific University, Washington School Research Center.

Anderman, L.H. and Anderman, E.M. (1999) 'Social predictors of changes in students' achievement goal orientations', *Contemporary Educational Psychology* 25, 1: 21–37.

Anderson, L.M., Brubaker, N.L., Alleman-Brooks, J. and Duffy, G.G. (1985) 'A qualitative study of seatwork in first grade classrooms', *Elementary School Journal* 86: 123–40.

Areglado, R.J., Bradley, R.C. and Lane, P.S. (1997) *Learning for Life: creating classrooms for self-directed learning*, Thousand Oaks, CA: Corwin Press.

Aronson, E. and Bridgeman, D. (1979) 'Jigsaw groups and the desegregated classroom: in pursuit of common goals', *Personality and Social Psychology Bulletin* 5: 438–46.

Aronson, E. and Patnoe, S. (1997) *The Jigsaw Classroom: building cooperation in the classroom*, New York: Allyn & Bacon.

Aronson, E., Blaney, N.T., Stephan, C., Rosenfield, R. and Sikes, J. (1977) 'Interdependence in the classroom: a field study', *Journal of Educational Psychology* 69: 121–8.

Atkinson, E.S. (1999) 'Key factors influencing pupil motivation in design and technology', *Journal of Technology Education* 10, 2: 4–26.

Axelrod, R. (1990) *The Evolution of Cooperation*, Harmondsworth: Penguin.

Bandura, A. (2000) 'Exercise of human agency through collective efficacy', *Current Directions in Psychological Science* 9, 3: 75–8.

Bartsch, K. and Wellman, H.M. (1995) *Children Talk about the Mind*, New York: Oxford University Press.

Battistich, V. (2001) 'Effects of an elementary school intervention on students' "connectedness" to school and social adjustment during middle school', unpublished paper presented at Symposium on resilience education at annual meeting of AERA, Seattle, WA.

Battistich, V. and Hom, A. (1997) 'The relationship between students' sense of their school as a community and their involvement in problem behaviors', *American Journal of Public Health* 87, 12: 1997–2001.

Battistich, V., Schaps, E., Watson, M. and Solomon, D. (1996) 'Prevention effects of the child development project: early findings from an ongoing multisite demonstration trial', *Journal of Adolescent Research* 11, 1: 12–35.

Battistich, V., Solomon, D., Kim, D., Watson, M. and Schaps, E. (1995) 'Schools as communities, poverty level of student populations, and students' attitudes, motives and performance: a multilevel analysis', *American Education Research Journal* 32, 3: 627–58.

Battistich, V., Solomon, D., Watson, M. and Schaps, E. (1994) 'Students and teachers in caring classroom and school communities', unpublished paper presented at Annual Meeting of AERA, New Orleans, LA.

Battistich, V., Solomon, D., Watson, M. and Schaps, E. (1997) 'Caring school communities', *Educational Psychologist* 32, 3: 137–51.

Battistich, V., Watson, M., Solomon, D., Lewis, C. and Schaps, E. (1999) 'Beyond the three r's: a broader agenda for school reform', *Elementary School Journal* 99, 5: 415–32.

Bayliss, V. (1999) *Opening Minds: education for the 21st century*, London: RSA.

Bayliss, V. and others (2002) *Opening Minds: project update*, London: RSA.

Benninga, J.S., Tracz, S.M., Sparks, R.K., Solomon, D., Battistich, V., Delucchi, K.L., Sandoval, R. and Stanley, B. (1991) 'Effects of two contrasting school task and incentive structures on children's social development', *Elementary School Journal* 92, 2: 149–67.

Bereiter, C. (2002a) 'Education in a knowledge society', in B. Smith (ed.) *Liberal Education in a Knowledge Society*, La Salle, IL: Open Court.

Bereiter, C. (2002b) *Education and Mind in a Knowledge Society*, Mahwah, NJ: Lawrence Erlbaum.

Bereiter, C., Scardamalia, M., Cassells, C. and Hewitt, J. (1997) 'Postmodernism, knowledge building, and elementary science', *Elementary School Journal* 97, 4: 329–40.

Bielaczyc, K. (2001) 'Designing social infrastructure: the challenge of building computer-supported learning communities', in P. Dillenbourg, A. Eurelings and K. Hakkarainen (eds) *European Perspectives on Computer-supported Collaborative Learning. The Proceedings of the First European Conference on Computer-supported Collaborative Learning*, Maastricht, Netherlands: University of Maastricht.

Bielaczyc, K. and Collins, A. (2000) 'Learning communities in classrooms: a reconceptualization of educational practice', in C.M. Reigeluth (ed.)

Instructional-design Theories and Models (Vol. II), Mahwah, NJ: Lawrence Erlbaum.

Blair, T. (1998) *The Third Way: new politics for the new century*, London: The Fabian Society.

Bloome, D., Puro, P. and Theodorou, E. (1989) 'Procedural display and classroom lessons', *Curriculum Inquiry* 19, 3: 265–91.

Boekaerts, M. (1999) 'Self-regulated learning: where we are today', *International Journal of Educational Research* 31, 6: 445–57.

Boekaerts, M. (2002) 'Bringing about change in the classroom: strengths and weaknesses of the self-regulated learning approach – EARLI Presidential Address, 2001', *Learning and Instruction* 12: 589–604.

Bohl, D. (ed.) (1994) *The Learning Organization in Action (Reprints from Organizational Dynamics)*, New York: American Management Association.

Bottery, M. (2003) 'The leadership of learning communities in a culture of unhappiness', *School Leadership and Management*, 23, 2: 187–207.

Broadfoot, P.M. (1987) 'Profiling and the affective curriculum', *Journal of Curriculum Studies* 19, 1: 25–34.

Brooks, J.G. and Brooks, M.G. (1999) *In Search of Understanding: the case for constructivist classrooms*, Alexandria, VA: Association for Supervision and Curriculum Development.

Brown, A.L. (1975) 'The development of memory: knowing, knowing about knowing, and knowing how to know', in H.W. Reese (ed.) *Advances in Child Development and Behavior*, New York: Academic Press.

Brown, A.L. (1997) 'Transforming schools into communities of thinking and learning about serious matters', *American Psychologist* 52, 4: 399–413.

Brown, A.L., Ash, D., Rutherford, M., Nakagawa, K., Gordon, A. and Campione, J.C. (1993) 'Distributed expertise in the classroom', in G. Salomon (ed.) *Distributed Cognitions: psychological and educational considerations*, New York: Cambridge University Press.

Brown, A.L. and Campione, J.C. (1994) 'Guided discovery in a community of learners', in K. McGilly (ed.) *Classroom Lessons: integrating cognitive theory and classroom practice*, Cambridge, MA: MIT Press.

Brown, A.L. and Campione, J.C. (1996) 'Psychological theory and the design of innovative learning environments: on procedures, principles, and systems', in L. Schauble and R. Glaser (ed.) *Innovations in Learning: new environments for education*, Hillsdale, NJ: Lawrence Erlbaum.

Brown, A.L. and Campione, J.C. (1998) 'Designing a community of young learners: theoretical and practical lessons', in N.M. Lambert and B.L. McCombs (eds) *How Students Learn: reforming schools through learner-centered education*, Washington, DC: American Psychological Association.

Brown, C.J. and Fouts, J.T. (2003) *Classroom Instruction in Achievers Grantee*

High Schools: a baseline report prepared for the Bill & Melinda Gates Foundation, Mill Creek, WA: Fouts & Associates.

Bryk, A.S. and Driscoll, M.E. (1988) *An Empirical Investigation of the School as a Community*, Chicago, IL: University of Chicago School of Education.

Bryk, A.S. and Schneider, B. (2002) *Trust in Schools: a core resource for improvement*, New York: Russell Sage Foundation.

Bryk, A.S., Camburn, E. and Louis, K.S. (1999) 'Professional community in Chicago elementary schools: facilitating factors and organizational consequences', *Educational Administration Quarterly* 35, Supplement: 751–81.

Bryk, A.S., Lee, V.E. and Holland, P.B. (1993) *Catholic Schools and the Common Good*, Cambridge, MA: Harvard University Press.

Bryk, A.S., Lee, V.E. and Smith, J.B. (1990) 'High school organization and its effects on teachers and students: an interpretative summary of the research', in W.H. Clune and J.F. Witte (eds) *Choice and Control in American Education*, Philadelphia, PA: Falmer Press.

Bryson, M. and Scardamalia, M. (1996) 'Fostering reflectivity in the argumentative thinking of students with different learning histories', *Reading and Writing Quarterly: Overcoming Learning Difficulties* 12: 351–84.

Campione, J., Shapiro, A.M. and Brown, A.L. (1995) 'Forms of transfer in a community of learners: flexible learning and understanding', in A. McKeough, J. Lupart and A. Marini (eds) *Teaching for Transfer: fostering generalization in learning*, Mahwah, NJ: Lawrence Erlbaum.

Caswell, B. and Bielaczyc, K. (2002) 'Knowledge Forum: altering the relationship between students and scientific knowledge', *Education, Communication and Information* 1, 3: 281–305.

Caswell, B. and Lamon, M. (1999) 'Development of scientific literacy: the evolution of ideas in a knowledge-building classroom', in J. Leach and B. Moon (eds) *Learners and Pedagogy*, London: Paul Chapman in association with Open University.

Christal, M., Ferneding, K., Puthoff, A.K. and Resta, P. (1997) *Schools as Knowledge-building Communities*, Denton, TX: Texas Center for Educational Technology.

Clarke, S., McCallum, B. and Lopez-Charles, G. (2001) *Gillingham Partnership Formative Assessment Project 2000–2001. Interim Report on the first term of the project: communicating learning intentions, developing success criteria and pupil self-evaluation*, London: University of London Institute of Education.

Clifford, M. (1990) 'Students need challenge, not easy success', *Educational Leadership* 48, 1: 22–5.

Clifford, M.M. (1988) 'Failure tolerance and academic risk-taking in ten- to twelve-year-old students', *British Journal of Educational Psychology* 58, 1: 15–27.

Cobb, P. and Bauersfeld, H. (eds) (1995) *The Emergence of Mathematical Meaning: interaction in classroom cultures*, Hillsdale, NJ: Lawrence Erlbaum.

Cohen, A. (1995) 'Mediated collaborative learning – how CSILE supports a shift from knowledge in the head to knowledge in the world', unpublished paper presented at Annual conference of AERA, San Francisco, CA.

Cohen, A. and Scardamalia, M. (1998) 'Discourse about ideas: monitoring and regulation in face-to-face and computer-mediated environments', *Interactive Learning Environments* 6, 1–2: 93–113.

Connell, J.P. and Wellborn, J.G. (1991) 'Competence, autonomy, and relatedness: a motivational analysis of self-system processes', in M.R. Gunnar and L.A. Sroufe (eds) *Self Processes and Development (Minnesota Symposium on Child Development Vol. 23)*, Hillsdale, NJ: Lawrence Erlbaum.

Connell, J.P., Halpern-Felsher, B.L., Clifford, E., Crichlow, W. and Usinger, P. (1995) 'Hanging in there: behavioral, psychological, and contextual factors affecting whether African-American adolescents stay in high-school', *Journal of Adolescent Research* 10, 1: 41–63.

Corrie, M., Haystead, J. and Zaklukiewicz, S. (1982) *Classroom Management Strategies: a study in secondary schools*, London: Hodder & Stoughton for the Scottish Council for Research in Education.

Crawford, B., Krajcik, J. and Marx, R. (1999) 'Elements of a community of learners in a middle school science classroom', *Science Education* 83, 6: 701–23.

Cuban, L. (1993a) 'Computers meet classroom – classroom wins', *Teachers College Record* 95, 2: 185–210.

Cuban, L. (1993b) *How Teachers Taught: constancy and change in American classrooms 1890–1990*, New York: Longman.

Cuttance, P. (1998) 'Quality assurance reviews as a catalyst for school improvement in Australia', in A. Hargreaves, A. Lieberman, M. Fullan and D. Hopkins (eds) *International Handbook of Educational Change (Part Two)*, Dordrecht, Netherlands: Kluwer.

Davis, E.A. (2003) 'Prompting middle school science students for productive reflection: generic and directed prompts', *Journal of the Learning Sciences* 12, 1: 91–142.

Dawes, L., Mercer, N. and Wegerif, R. (2000) *Thinking Together: activities for teachers and children at Key Stage 2*, Birmingham: Questions Publishing.

Deci, E.L. and Ryan, R.M. (1982) 'Intrinsic motivation to teach: possibilities and obstacles in our colleges and universities', in J. Bess (ed.) *New Directions for Learning and Teaching: motivating professors to teach effectively*, San Francisco, CA: Jossey Bass.

Deci, E., Koestner, R. and Ryan, R. (1999) 'A meta-analytic review of experiments examining the effects of extrinsic rewards on intrinsic motivation', *Psychological Bulletin* 125, 6: 627–68.

Deci, E.L., Spiegel, N.H., Ryan, R.M., Koestner, R. and Kauffmann, M. (1982) 'The effects of performance standards on teaching styles: the behavior of controlling teachers', *Journal of Educational Psychology* 74: 852–9.

Deci, E.L., Vallerand, R.J., Pelletier, L.G. and Ryan, R.M. (1991) 'Motivation and education: the self-determination perspective', *Educational Psychologist* 26, 3&4: 325–46.

Dennison, B. and Kirk, R. (1990) *Do Review Learn Apply: a simple guide to experiential learning*, Oxford: Blackwell.

Dewey, J. (1916) *Democracy and Education: an introduction to the philosophy of education*, New York: Macmillan.

Dietz, T. and Burns, T.R. (1992) 'Human agency and the evolutionary dynamics of culture', *Acta Sociologica* 35, 3: 187–200.

Dixon, N.M. (1998) *Dialogue at Work: making talk developmental for people and organizations*, London: Lemos & Crane.

Donoahue, Z. (2003) 'Science teaching and learning: teachers and children plan together', *Networks Journal* 6, 1.

Donoahue, Z., Patterson, L. and Van Tassell, M.A. (eds) (1996) *Research in the Classroom: talk, texts, & inquiry*, Newark, DE: International Reading Association.

Doyle, W. (1983) 'Academic work', *Review of Educational Research* 53, 2: 159–99.

Doyle, W. (1984) 'How order is achieved in classrooms: an interim report', *Journal of Curriculum Studies* 16, 3: 259–77.

Doyle, W. (1986) 'Classroom organization and management', in M.C. Wittrock (ed.) *Handbook of Research on Teaching*, New York: Macmillan.

Doyle, W. (1990) 'Classroom knowledge as a foundation for teaching', *Teachers College Record* 91, 3: 347–60.

Driver, R., Asoko, H., Leach, J., Mortimer, E. and Scott, P. (1994) 'Constructing scientific knowledge in the classroom', *Educational Researcher* 23, 7: 5–12.

Dweck, C.S. (1991) 'Self-theories and goals: their role in personality, motivation and development', in R. Dienstbier (ed.) *Nebraska Symposium on Motivation. Vol. 40: Developmental perspectives on motivation*, Lincoln, NE: University of Nebraska Press.

Eckert, P., Goldman, S. and Wenger, E. (1996) 'The school as a community of engaged learners', *Wingspread Journal* 9, 3: 4–6.

Elbers, E. (2003) 'Classroom interaction as reflection: learning and teaching mathematics in a community of inquiry', *Educational Studies in Mathematics* 54, 1: 77–99.

Elbers, E. and Streefland, L. (2000a) '"Shall we be researchers again?" Identity and social interaction in a community of inquiry', in H. Cowie and D. van der Aalsvoort (eds) *Social Interaction in Learning and Instruction: the meaning of discourse for the construction of knowledge*, Oxford: Pergamon.

Elbers, E. and Streefland, L. (2000b) 'Collaborative learning and the construction of common knowledge', *European Journal of Psychology of Education* 15, 4: 479–90.

Engle, R.A. and Conant, F.R. (2002) 'Guiding principles for fostering productive disciplinary engagement: explaining an emergent argument in a community of learners classroom', *Cognition and Instruction* 20, 4: 399–484.

Featherstone, D., Munby, H. and Russell, T. (1997) *Finding a Voice while Learning to Teach: others' voices can help you find your own*, London: Falmer Press.

Fiol, M. (1996) 'Consensus, diversity, and learning in organizations', in J. Meindl, C. Stubbart and J. Porac (eds) *Cognition within and between Organizations*, London: Sage.

Flavell, J.H. (1976) 'Metacognitive aspects of problem-solving', in L.B. Resnick (ed.) *The Nature of Intelligence*, Hillsdale, NJ: Lawrence Erlbaum.

Forman, E. and Ansell, E. (2001) 'The multiple voices of a mathematics classroom community', *Educational Studies in Mathematics* 46, 1/3: 115–42.

Freire, P. (1970) *Pedagogia del Oprimido*, Montevideo: Tierra Nueva; trans. M.B. Ramos (1972) *Pedagogy of the Oppressed*, Harmondsworth: Penguin.

Galton, M. and Williamson, J. (1992) *Group Work in the Primary Classroom*, London: Routledge.

Gergen, K.J. (1991) *The Saturated Self: dilemmas of identity in contemporary life*, New York: Basic Books.

Gibbs, G. (1988) *Learning by Doing: a guide to teaching and learning methods*, London: Further Education Unit.

Goddard, R., Hoy, W. and Hoy, A. (2000) 'Collective teacher efficacy: its meaning, measure and impact on student achievement', *American Educational Research Journal* 7, 5/6: 439–54.

Gokhale, A.A. (1995) 'Collaborative learning enhances critical thinking', *Journal of Technology Education* 7, 1.

Goodenow, C. (1992) 'School motivation, engagement, and sense of belonging among urban adolescent students', unpublished paper presented at Annual Meeting of AERA, San Francisco, CA.

Goodenow, C. and Grady, K.E. (1993) 'The relationship of school belonging and friends: values to academic motivation among urban adolescent students', *Journal of Experimental Education* 62, 1: 60–71.

Gray, J. (2000) 'How schools learn: common concerns and different responses', *Research Papers in Education* 15, 3: 235–9.

Gray, J., Hopkins, D., Reynolds, D., Wilcox, B., Farrell, S. and Jesson, D. (1999) *Improving Schools: performance and potential*, Buckingham: Open University Press.

Gromyko, Y. and Maurice, H.S. (2000) 'Constructions of community: aspects of cultural historical study of school curriculum', *Discourse: Studies in the Cultural Politics of Education* 21, 2: 193–204.

Hagborg, W. (1998) 'An investigation of a brief measure of school membership', *Adolescence* 33, 130: 461–8.

Hakkarainen, K. (1995) 'Collaborative inquiry in the computer-supported intentional learning environments', unpublished paper presented at Annual Conference of the European Association for Research on Learning and Instruction, University of Nijmegen, Netherlands.

Hakkarainen, K. (2003) 'Emergence of progressive-inquiry culture in computer-supported collaborative learning', *Learning Environments Research* 6, 2: 199–220.

Hakkarainen, K. and Sintonen, M. (2002) 'Interrogative model of inquiry and computer supported collaborative learning', *Science and Education* 11, 1: 25–43.

Hall, K., Bowman, H. and Myers, J. (1999) 'Metacognition and reading awareness among samples of nine-year-olds in two cities', *Educational Research* 41, 1: 99–107.

Haneda, M. and Wells, G. (2000) 'Writing in knowledge-building communities', *Research in the Teaching of English* 34, 3: 430–57.

Hannikainen, M. and van Oers, B. (1999) 'Signs and problems of togetherness in a community of learners', unpublished paper presented at Annual EECERA (European Early Childhood Education Research Association) Ninth Conference, Helsinki, Finland

Harré, R. and Langenhove, L.V. (eds) (1999) *Positioning Theory: moral contexts of intentional action*, Oxford: Blackwell.

Harvey-Jones, J. (1995) *All Together Now*, London: Mandarin Books.

Heald-Taylor, B.G. (1996) 'Three paradigms for literature instruction in Grades 3 to 6', *The Reading Teacher* 49, 6: 456–65.

Hewitt, J. and Scardamalia, M. (1996) 'Design principles for the support of distributed processes', unpublished paper presented at Annual Meeting of the American Educational Research Association, New York City.

Hewitt, R., Epstein, D., Leonard, D., Mauthner, M. and Watkins, C. (2003) *The Violence-resilient School: a comparative study of schools and their environments*, ESRC Violence Research Programme.

Hill, P. (1998) 'Shaking the foundations: research driven school reform', *School Effectiveness and School Improvement* 9, 4: 419–36.

Hipp, K.A. and Huffman, J.B. (2000) 'How leadership is shared and visions emerge in the creation of learning communities', unpublished paper presented at Annual Meeting of the American Educational Research Association, New Orleans, LA.

Hogan, K. (2001) 'Collective metacognition: the interplay of individual, social and cultural meaning in small groups' reflective thinking', in F. Columbus (ed.) *Advances in Psychology Research (Vol. 7)*, Huntington, NY: Nova Science Publishers.

Holliday, D.C. (2002) *Jigsaw IV: using student/teacher concerns to improve Jigsaw III*, ERIC document ED465687, Indiana University Northwest.

Huffman, J.B. and Hipp, K.A. (2000) 'Creating communities of learners: the interaction of shared leadership, shared vision, and supportive conditions', unpublished paper presented at Annual Meeting of the American Educational Research Association, New Orleans, LA.

Hughes, M. (1997) *Lessons Are For Learning*, Stafford: Network Educational Press.

Hume, K. (2000) 'Seeing shades of grey: developing a knowledge-building community through science', in G. Wells (ed.) *Action, Talk, and Text: learning and teaching through inquiry*, New York: Teachers College Press.

Inagaki, K., Hatano, G. and Morita, E. (1998) 'Construction of mathematical knowledge through whole-class discussion', *Learning and Instruction* 8, 6: 503–26.

International Baccalaureate Organisation (2001) *Primary Years Programme Monograph*, Geneva: IBO.

Israelashvili, M. (1997) 'School adjustment, school membership and adolescents' future expectations', *Journal of Adolescence* 20, 5: 525–35.

Jalongo, M.R. (1991) *Creating Learning Communities: the role of the teacher in the 21st century*, Bloomington, IN: National Educational Service.

Johnson, B. (2003) 'Teacher collaboration: good for some, not so good for others', *Educational Studies* 29, 4: 337–50.

Johnson, D.W., Johnson, R.T. and Holubec, E.J. (1994) *Cooperative Learning in the Classroom*, Alexandria, VA: ASCD.

Johnson, L., Lutzow, J., Strothoff, M. and Zannis, C. (1995) *Reducing Negative Behavior by Establishing Helping Relationships and a Community Identity Program*, Rockford, IL:

Johnson, S.M. (1990) *Teachers at Work: achieving success in our schools*, New York: Basic Books.

Kitayama, S., Markus, H., Matsumoto, H. and Norasakkunkit, V. (1997) 'Individual and collective processes in the construction of the self: self-enhancement in the United States and self-criticism in Japan', *Journal of Personality and Social Psychology* 72, 6: 1245–67.

Knight, G.P. and Bohlmeyer, E.M. (1990) 'Cooperative learning and achievement: methods for assessing causal mechanisms', in S. Sharan (ed.) *Cooperative Learning: theory and research*, New York: Praeger.

Kohn, A. (1996) *Beyond Discipline: from compliance to community*, Alexandria, VA: Association for Supervision and Curriculum Development.

Kolb, D.A. (1984) *Experiential Learning: experience as the source of learning and development*, Englewood Cliffs, NJ: Prentice-Hall.

Kruse, S.D., Louis, K.S. and Bryk, A.S. (1994) 'Building professional community in schools', in Center on Organization and Restructuring of Schools (ed.) *Issues in Restructuring Schools No. 6*, Madison, WI: University of Wisconsin-Madison.

Kruse, S.D., Louis, K.S. and Bryk, A.S. (1995) 'An emerging framework for analyzing school-based professional community', in K.S. Louis, S.D. Kruse and Associates (eds) *Professionalism and Community: perspectives on reforming urban schools*, Thousand Oaks, CA: Corwin.

Kyriakides, L., Campbell, R. and Gagatsis, A. (2000) 'The significance of the classroom effect in primary schools: an application of Creemers' comprehensive model of educational effectiveness', *School Effectiveness and School Improvement* 11, 4: 501–29.

Labaree, D.F. (1997) *How to Succeed in School – Without Really Learning: the credentials race in American education*, New Haven, CT: Yale University Press.

Lamon, M., Chan, C., Scardamalia, M., Burtis, P.J. and Brett, C. (1993) 'Beliefs about learning and constructive processes in reading: effects of a computer supported intentional learning environment (CSILE)', unpublished paper presented at Annual meeting of AERA, Atlanta, GA.

Lamon, M., Reeve, R. and Scardamalia, M. (2001) 'Mapping learning and the growth of knowledge in a knowledge building community', unpublished paper presented at Annual Meeting of AERA, Seattle, WA

Latour, B. and Woolgar, S. (1992) *Laboratory Life: the social construction of scientific facts*, Princeton, NJ: Princeton University Press.

Lee, V.E. and Smith, J.B. (1995) 'Effects of high-school restructuring and size on early gains in achievement and engagement', *Sociology of Education* 68, 4: 241–70.

Lee, V.E. and Smith, J.B. (1996) 'Collective responsibility for learning and its effects on gains in achievement for early secondary school students', *American Journal of Education* 104, 2: 103–47.

Lee, V.E., Smith, J.B. and Croninger, R.G. (1995) 'Another look at high-school restructuring: more evidence that it improves student achievement and more insight into why', *Center on Organization and Restructuring of Schools 'Issues in restructuring schools'*, 9, Fall: 1–10.

Leithwood, K. and Jantzi, D. (2000) 'The effects of transformational leadership on organizational conditions and student engagement with school', *Journal of Educational Administration* 38, 2: 112–29.

Leithwood, K.A. and Louis, K.S. (eds) (1998) *Organizational Learning in Schools*, Lisse, Netherlands: Swets & Zeitlinger.

Leithwood, K., Steinbach, R. and Ryan, S. (1997) 'Leadership and team learning in secondary schools', *School Leadership and Management* 17, 3: 303–25.

Levine, D.A. (2003) *Building Classroom Communities: strategies for developing a culture of caring*, Bloomington, IN: National Education Services.

Lewis, C., Schaps, E. and Watson, M.S. (1996) 'The caring classroom's academic edge', *Educational Leadership* 54, 1: 16–21.

Lipponen, L. (2002) 'Exploring foundations for computer-supported collaborative learning', in G. Stahl (ed.) *Computer-supported Collaborative Learning: foundations for a CSCL community, Proceedings of the Computer-supported Collaborative Learning 2002 Conference*, Mahwah, NJ: Lawrence Erlbaum.

Little, J.W. (1988) 'Assessing the prospects for teacher leadership', in A. Lieberman (ed.) *Building a Professional Culture in Schools*, New York: Teachers College Press.

Lou, Y.P., Abrami, P.C., Spence, J.C., Poulsen, C., Chambers, B. and d'Apollonia, S. (1996) 'Within-class grouping: a meta-analysis', *Review of Educational Research* 66, 4: 423–58.

Louis, K.S. and Marks, H. (1998) 'Does professional community affect the classroom? teachers' work and student experiences in restructured schools', *American Journal of Education* 106, 4: 532–75.

Marble, S., Finley, S. and Ferguson, C. (2000) *Understanding Teachers' Perspectives on Teaching and Learning: a synthesis of work in five study sites*, ERIC document ED449155, Austin, TX: Southwest Educational Developmental Laboratory.

Markus, H. and Kitayama, S. (1994) 'A collective fear of the collective – implications for selves and theories of selves', *Personality and Social Psychology Bulletin* 20, 5: 568–79.

Markus, H.R. and Kitayama, S. (1991) 'Culture and the self: implications for cognition, emotion, and motivation', *Psychological Review* 98, 2: 224–53.

Marx, K. (1939) *Grundrisse der Kritik der politischen Oekonomie*, Moscow: Institute for Marxism-Leninism; trans. Martin Nicolaus (1973) *Grundrisse: foundations of the critique of political economy*, Harmondsworth: Penguin.

Marzano, R.J. (1998) *A Theory-based Meta-analysis of Research on Instruction*, http://www.mcrel.org/products/learning/meta.pdf, Aurora, CO: Mid-continent Regional Educational Laboratory.

Mason, L. (1998) 'Sharing cognition to construct scientific knowledge in school context: the role of oral and written discourse', *Instructional Science* 26: 359–89.

McNeil, L.M. (2000) *Contradictions of School Reform: educational costs of standardized testing*, New York: Routledge.

Meece, J.L. and Miller, S.D. (1999) 'Changes in elementary school children's achievement goals for reading and writing: results of a longitudinal and an intervention study', *Scientific Studies of Reading* 3, 3: 207–29.

Meehan, S., Holmes, B. and Tangney, B. (2001) 'Who wants to be a teacher? An exploration of the theory of communal constructivism at the chalk face', *Teacher Development* 5, 2: 177–90.

Mercer, N. (2002) 'Developing dialogues', in G. Wells and G. Claxton (eds) *Learning for Life in the 21st Century: sociocultural perspectives on the future of education*, Oxford: Blackwell.

Miller, S.D. and Meece, J.L. (1999) 'Third graders' motivational preferences for reading and writing tasks', *Elementary School Journal* 100, 1: 19–35.

Mitchell, C. and Sackney, L. (2000) *Profound Improvement: building capacity for a learning community*, Lisse, Netherlands: Swets & Zeitlinger.

Miyake, N. and Koschmann, T. (2002) 'Realization of CSCL conversations: technology transfer and the CSILE project', in T. Koschmann, N. Miyake and R. Hall (eds) *CSCL2: carrying forward the conversation*, Mahwah, NJ: Lawrence Erlbaum.

Moore, P. and Scevak, J. (1995) 'The effects of strategy training on high school students' learning from science texts', *European Journal of Psychology of Education* 10, 4: 401–9.

Morgan, G. (1988) *Images of Organisation*, London: Sage.

Muijs, D. and Reynolds, D. (2001) *Effective Teaching: evidence and practice*, London: Paul Chapman.

Mulford, B. and Silins, H. (2003) 'Leadership for organisational learning and improved student outcomes – what do we know?', *Cambridge Journal of Education* 33, 2: 175–95.

Munro, J. (1999) 'Learning more about learning improves teacher effectiveness', *School Effectiveness and School Improvement* 10, 2: 151–71.

Nicholls, J.G. and Thorkildsen, T.A. (eds) (1995) *Reasons for Learning: expanding the conversation on student–teacher collaboration*, New York: Teachers College Press.

OECD (2001a) *Schooling for Tomorrow: what schools for the future?*, 92-64-19526-2, Paris: OECD (Organisation for Economic Co-operation and Development) Centre for Educational Research and Innovation.

OECD (2001b) *Knowledge and Skills for Life: first results from the OECD 'Programme for International Student Assessment' (PISA) 2000*, Paris: Organisation for Economic Co-operation and Development.

Office for Standards in Education (2002) *The Curriculum in Successful Primary Schools (Survey Report HMI 553)*, London: Ofsted.

Office for Standards in Education (2003) *Inspecting Schools: framework for inspecting schools*, London: Ofsted.

Orr, J.E. (1997) *Talking about Machines: an ethnography of a modern job*, Ithaca, NY: Cornell University Press.

Osterman, K.F. (1998) 'Student community within the school context: a research synthesis', unpublished paper presented at Annual Meeting of the American Educational Research Association, San Diego, CA.

Osterman, K.F. (2000) 'Students' need for belonging in the school community', *Review of Educational Research* 70, 3: 323–67.

Paavola, S., Lipponen, L. and Hakkarainen, K. (2002) 'Epistemological foundations for CSCL: a comparison of three models of innovative knowledge communities', in G. Stahl (ed.) *Computer-supported Collaborative Learning: Foundations for a CSCL community, Proceedings of the Computer-supported Collaborative Learning 2002 Conference*, Mahwah, NJ: Lawrence Erlbaum.

Palincsar, A.S. and Brown, A.L. (1984) 'Reciprocal teaching of comprehension-fostering and monitoring activities', *Cognition and Instruction* 1, 2: 117–75.

Palincsar, A.S., Magnusson, S.J., Marano, N., Ford, D. and Brown, N. (1998) 'Designing a community of practice: principles and practice of the GIsML Community', *Teaching and Teacher Education* 14: 5–19.

Paradise, R. (1998) 'What's different about learning in schools as compared to family and community settings?', *Human Development* 41, 4: 270–8.

Paris, S.G. and Paris, A.H. (2001) 'Classroom applications of research on self-regulated learning', *Educational Psychologist* 36, 2: 89–101.

Perkins, D.N. (1994) 'Thinking-centered learning', *Educational Leadership* 51, 4: 84–5.

Perry, N.E. (1998) 'Young children's self-regulated learning and contexts that support it', *Journal of Educational Psychology* 90, 4: 715–29.

Peterson, P.L., Carpenter, T.P. and Fennema, E. (1989) 'Teachers' knowledge of students' knowledge in mathematics problem-solving: correlational and case analyses', *Journal of Educational Psychology* 81: 558–69.

Powell, S.D. and Makin, M. (1994) 'Enabling pupils with learning difficulties to reflect on their own thinking', *British Educational Research Journal* 20, 5: 579–93.

Prawat, R.S. (1992) 'From individual differences to learning communities – our changing focus', *Educational Leadership* April: 9–13.

Prawat, R.S. and Peterson, P.L. (1999) 'Social constructivist views of learning', in J. Murphy and K.S. Louis (eds) *Handbook of Research on Educational Administration*, 2nd edn, San Francisco, CA: Jossey-Bass.

Rafal, C.T. (1996) 'From co-construction to take-overs: science talk in a group of four girls', *Journal of the Learning Sciences* 5, 3: 279–93.

Rait, E. (1995) 'Against the current: organizational learning in schools', in S.B. Bacharach and B. Mundell (ed.) *Images of Schools: structures and roles in organizational behavior*, London: Sage.

Reed, J. and Stoll, L. (2000) 'Promoting organisational learning in schools – the role of feedback', in S. Askew (ed.) *Feedback for Learning*, London: Routledge.

Resnick, M.D., Bearman, P.S., Blum, R.W., Bauman, K.E., Harris, K.M., Jones, J., Tabor, J., Beuhring, T., Sieving, R.E., Shew, M., Ireland, M., Bearinger, L.H. and Udry, J.R. (1997) 'Protecting adolescents from harm: findings from the National Longitudinal Study on Adolescent Health', *Journal of the American Medical Association* 278, 10: 823–32.

Resnick, M.D., Harris, L. and Blum, R. (1993) *The Impact of Caring and Connectedness on Adolescent Health and Well-being*, Minneapolis, MN: University of Minnesota Children Youth and Family Consortium.

Roeser, R., Midgley, C. and Urdan, T. (1996) 'Perceptions of the school psychological environment and early adolescents' psychological and behavioral functioning in school: the mediating role of goals and belonging', *Journal of Educational Psychology* 88, 3: 408–22.

Rosenholtz, S.J. (1991) *Teachers' Workplace: the social organization of schools*, New York: Teachers College Press.

Rosenshine, B. and Meister, C. (1994) 'Reciprocal teaching: a review of the research', *Review of Educational Research* 64, 4: 479–530.

RSA (2003) *Opening Minds: what we have learned*, London: RSA.

Russell, B. (1930) 'Homogeneous America', *Outlook and Independent* 154, 19 February: 285–7 and 318. Reprinted as 'Modern homogeneity' in *In Praise of Idleness, and Other Essays*, London: Allen & Unwin, 1935; and in *Let the People Think: a selection of essays*, London: Watts & Co., 1941 [2nd edition, London: The Rationalist Press, *c.* 1961].

Rutter, M., Maughan, B., Mortimore, P. and Ouston, J. (1979) *Fifteen Thousand Hours: secondary schools and their effects*, Wells: Open Books.

Ryan, R.M. (1995) 'Psychological needs and the facilitation of integrative processes', *Journal of Personality* 63, 3: 397–427.

Ryan, R.M. and Deci, E.L. (2000) 'Intrinsic and extrinsic motivations: classic definitions and new directions', *Contemporary Educational Psychology* 25: 54–67.

Ryser, G., Beeler, J. and McKenzie, C. (1995) 'Effects of a Computer-Supported Intentional Learning Environment (CSILE) on students' self-concept, self-regulatory behavior, and critical thinking ability', *Journal of Educational Computing Research* 13, 4: 375–85.

Sarason, S.B. (1993) *The Predictable Failure of Educational Reform: can we change course before it's too late?*, San Francisco, CA: Jossey-Bass.

Scardamalia, M. (2002) 'Collective cognitive responsibility for the advancement of knowledge', in B. Smith (ed.) *Liberal Education in a Knowledge Society*, Chicago, IL: Open Court.

Scardamalia, M. (2003) 'CSILE/Knowledge Forum', in A. Kovalchick and K. Dawson (eds) *Education and Technology: an encyclopedia*, Santa Barbara, CA: ABC-CLIO Publishing.

Scardamalia, M. and Bereiter, C. (1991) 'Higher levels of agency for children in knowledge building: a challenge for the design of new knowledge media', *Journal of the Learning Sciences* 1, 1: 37–68.

Scardamalia, M. and Bereiter, C. (1992) 'Text-based and knowledge-based questioning by children', *Cognition and Instruction* 9, 3: 177–99.

Scardamalia, M. and Bereiter, C. (1994) 'Computer support for knowledge-building communities', *Journal of the Learning Sciences* 3, 3: 265–83.

Scardamalia, M. and Bereiter, C. (1996) 'Student communities for the advancement of knowledge', *Communications of the ACM* 39, 4: 36–7.

Scardamalia, M. and Bereiter, C. (1999) 'Schools as knowledge building organizations', in D. Keating and C. Hertzman (eds) *Today's Children, Tomorrow's Society: the developmental health and wealth of nations*, New York: Guilford Press.

Scardamalia, M., Bereiter, C. and Lamon, M. (1994) 'The CSILE Project: trying to bring the classroom into world 3', in K. McGilly (ed.) *Classroom Lessons: integrating cognitive theory and classroom practice*, Cambridge, MA: MIT Press.

Schaps, E. (2003) 'Creating a school community', *Educational Leadership* 60, 6: 31–3.

Schaps, E. and Lewis, C. (1999) 'Perils on an essential journey: building school community', *Phi Delta Kappan* 81, 3: 215–18.

Schaps, E. and Solomon, D. (1990) 'Schools and classrooms as caring communities', *Educational Leadership* 48, 3: 38–42.

Schaps, E. and Solomon, D. (2003) 'The role of the school's social environment in preventing student drug use', *Journal of Primary Prevention* 23, 3: 299–328.

Schaps, E., Battistich, V. and Solomon, D. (1997) 'School as a caring community: a key to character education', in A. Molnar (ed.) *The Construction of Children's Character, Part II: 96th yearbook of the National Society for the Study of Education*, Chicago, IL: University of Chicago Press.

Schlechty, P.C. (1990) *Schools for the Twenty-first Century: leadership imperatives for school reform*, San Francisco, CA: Jossey-Bass.

Schwartz, D.L. (1995) 'The emergence of abstract representations in dyad problem solving', *Journal of the Learning Sciences* 4, 3: 321–54.

Schwartz, D.L. and Lin, X. (2001) 'Computers, productive agency, and the effort toward shared meaning', *Journal of Computing in Higher Education* 12, 2: 3–33.

Scribner, J.P., Cockrell, K.S., Cockrell, D.H. and Valentine, J.W. (1999) 'Creating professional communities in schools through organizational learning: an evaluation of a school improvement process', *Educational Administration Quarterly* 35, 1: 130–60.

Senge, P.M. (1990) *The Fifth Discipline: the art and practice of the learning organisation*, London: Century Business.

Sergiovanni, T.J. (1994) *Building Community in Schools*, San Francisco, CA: Jossey-Bass.

Sfard, A. (1998) 'On two metaphors for learning and the dangers of choosing just one', *Educational Researcher* 27, 2: 4–13.

Sharan, Y. and Sharan, S. (eds) (1992) *Expanding Cooperative Learning through Group Investigation*, New York: Teachers College Press.

Shields, C.M. (1999) 'Learning from students about representation, identity, and community', *Educational Administration Quarterly* 35, 1: 106–29.

Short, K.G. (1990) 'Creating a community of learners', in K.G. Short and K.M. Pierce (eds) *Talking About Books: creating literate communities*, Portsmouth, NH: Heinemann.

Short, K.G. and Burke, C.L. (1991) *Creating Curriculum: teachers and students as a community of learners*, Portsmouth, NH: Heinemann.

Silins, H., Zarins, S. and Mulford, B. (2002) 'What characteristics and processes define a school as a learning organisation? Is this a useful concept to apply to schools?', *International Education Journal* 3, 1: 24–32.

Slavin, R.E. (1987) *Cooperative Learning: student teams, what research says to teachers*, Washington, DC: National Education Association.

Solomon, D., Battistich, V., Kim, D.-I. and Watson, M. (1997) 'Teacher practices associated with students' sense of the classroom as a community', *Social Psychology of Education* 1, 3: 235–67.

Solomon, D., Schaps, E., Watson, M. and Battistich, V. (1992) 'Creating caring school and classroom communities for all students', in R.A. Villa, J.S. Thousand, W. Stainback and S. Stainback (eds) *Restructuring for Caring and Effective Education: an administrative guide to creating heterogeneous schools*, Baltimore, MD: Paul H. Brookes.

Solomon, D., Watson, M., Battistich, V., Schaps, E. and Delucchi, K. (1992) 'Creating a caring community: educational practices that promote children's prosocial development', in F.K. Oeser, A. Dick and J.-L. Patry (eds) *Effective and Responsible Teaching: the new synthesis*, San Francisco, CA: Jossey Bass.

Solomon, D., Watson, M., Battistich, V., Schaps, E. and Delucchi, K. (1996) 'Creating classrooms that students experience as communities', *American Journal of Community Psychology* 24, 6: 719–48.

Spillane, J.P., Halverson, R. and Diamond, J.B. (2004) 'Towards a theory of leadership practice: a distributed perspective', *Journal of Curriculum Studies* 36, 1: 3–34.

Starnes, B.A. and Paris, C. (2000) 'Choosing to learn', *Phi Delta Kappan* January: 392–7.

Staub, F.C. and Stern, E. (2002) 'The nature of teachers' pedagogical content beliefs matters for students' achievement gains: quasi-experimental evidence from elementary mathematics', *Journal of Educational Psychology* 94, 2: 344–55.

Steinbrink, J., Walkiewicz, S. and Stahl, R.J. (1995) 'Jigsaw III = Jigsaw II + Cooperative test review: applications to the Language Arts classroom', in R.J. Stahl (ed.) *Learning in Language Arts: a handbook for teachers*, New York: Addison-Wesley.

Stodolsky, S.S. and Grossman, P.L. (2000) 'Changing students, changing teaching', *Teachers College Record* 102, 1: 125–72.

Stoll, L. (1999) 'Realising our potential: understanding and developing capacity for lasting improvement', *School Effectiveness and School Improvement* 10, 4: 503–32.

Stoll, L., Fink, D. and Earl, L. (2004) *It's about Learning (and it's about time)*, London: RoutledgeFalmer.

Sullivan, J. (2000) 'Stand and deliver – the teacher's integrity?', in C. Watkins, C. Lodge and R. Best (eds) *Tomorrow's Schools – towards integrity*, London: Routledge.

Supovitz, J.A. (2002) 'Developing communities of instructional practice', *Teachers College Record* 104, 8: 1591–626.

Thomas, G.P. (2003) 'Conceptualisation, development and validation of an instrument for investigating the metacognitive orientation of science classroom learning environments: the Metacognitive Orientation Learning Environment Scale – Science (MOLES-S)', *Learning Environments Research* 6, 2: 175–97.

Tönnies, F. (1887) *Gemeinschaft und Gesellschaft*, trans. C.P. Loomis (1957) *Community and Society*, New York: HarperCollins.

Turner, J. (1995) 'The influence of classroom contexts on young children's motivation for literacy', *Reading Research Quarterly* 30, 3: 410–41.

Van Tassell, M.A. (2000) 'Student inquiry in science: asking questions, building foundations, and making connections', in G. Wells (ed.) *Action, Talk, and Text: learning and teaching through inquiry*, New York: Teachers College Press.

van Zee, E. and Minstrell, J. (1997a) 'Using questioning to guide student thinking', *Journal of the Learning Sciences* 6, 2: 227–69.

van Zee, E. and Minstrell, J. (1997b) 'Reflective discourse: developing shared understandings in a physics classroom', *International Journal of Science Education* 19, 2: 209–28.

Voelkl, K. (1997) 'Identification with school', *American Journal of Education* 105, 3: 294–318.

Wagner, P. and Watkins, C. (2005) 'Narrative work in schools', in A. Vetere and E. Dowling (eds) *Narrative Therapies with Children and their Families: a practitioners' guide to concepts and approaches*, London: Brunner-Routledge.

Waldrop, M.M. (1994) *Complexity: the emerging science at the edge of order and chaos*, Harmondsworth: Penguin.

Wang, M., Haertel, G. and Walberg, H. (1990) 'What influences learning: a content analysis of review literature', *Journal of Educational Research* 84, 1: 30–43.

Wang, M.C., Haertel, G.D. and Walberg, H.J. (1994) 'What helps students learn?', *Educational Leadership* 51, 4: 74–9.

Watkins, C. (1998) *Managing Classroom Behaviour: a bit like air traffic control*, London: Association for Teachers and Lecturers.

Watkins, C. (2000a) *Managing Classroom Behaviour: from research to diagnosis*, London: Institute of Education.

Watkins, C. (2000b) 'Feedback between teachers', in S. Askew (ed.) *Feedback for Learning*, London: Routledge.

Watkins, C. (2001) *Learning about Learning enhances Performance*, London: Institute of Education School Improvement Network (Research Matters series, No. 13).

Watkins, C. (2003a) 'Connected school – learning school', unpublished paper presented at Annual Conference of the National Association for Pastoral Care in Education, Nottingham.

Watkins, C. (2003b) *Learning: a sense-maker's guide*, London: Association of Teachers and Lecturers.

Watkins, C. (2004a) 'Reclaiming pastoral care', *Pastoral Care in Education* 22, 2: 3–6.

Watkins, C. (2004b) 'Learning and leading', in National College for School Leadership (ed.) *Learning Texts*, Nottingham: NCSL.

Watkins, C. and Wagner, P. (2000) *Improving School Behaviour*, London: Paul Chapman/Sage.

Watkins, C. and Whalley, C. (1993) *Mentoring: resources for school-based development*, Harlow: Longman.

Watkins, C., Carnell, E., Lodge, C., Wagner, P. and Whalley, C. (1998) *Learning about Learning*, Coventry: National Association for Pastoral Care in Education.

Watkins, C., Carnell, E., Lodge, C., Wagner, P. and Whalley, C. (2000) *Learning about Learning: resources for supporting effective learning*, London: Routledge.

Watkins, C., Carnell, E., Lodge, C., Wagner, P. and Whalley, C. (2002) *Effective Learning*, London: Institute of Education School Improvement Network (Research Matters series, No. 17).

Watkins, C., Mauthner, M., Hewitt, R., Epstein, D. and Leonard, D. (2005) 'School violence, school differences and school discourses', submitted to *British Educational Research Journal*.

Watkins, D. (2000) 'Learning and teaching: a cross-cultural perspective', *School Leadership and Management* 20, 2: 161–73.

Watkins, K.E. and Marsick, V.J. (1993) *Sculpting the Learning Organization: lessons in the art and science of systemic change*, San Francisco, CA: Jossey-Bass.

Watkins, K.E. and Marsick, V.J. (eds) (1996) *Creating the Learning Organization*, Alexandria, VA: American Society for Training and Development.

Watkins, P. (1996) 'Decentralising education to the point of production: Sloanism, the market, and schools of the future', *Discourse: Studies in the Cultural Politics of Education* 17, 1: 85–99.

Wegerif, R. and Dawes, L. (2004) *Thinking and Learning with ICT: raising achievement in primary classrooms*, London: RoutledgeFalmer.

Wegerif, R. and Mercer, N. (1997) 'A dialogical framework for researching peer talk', in R. Wegerif and P. Scrimshaw (eds) *Computers and Talk in the Primary Classroom*, Clevedon: Multilingual Matters.

Weimer, M. (2002) *Learner Centered Teaching: five key changes to practice*, San Francisco, CA: Jossey-Bass.

Wells, G. (1999) *Dialogic Inquiry: towards a sociocultural practice and theory of education*, Cambridge: Cambridge University Press.

Wells, G. (2000) 'The case for dialogic inquiry', in G. Wells (ed.) *Action, Talk, and Text: learning and teaching through inquiry*, New York: Teachers College Press.

Wells, G. (2002a) 'Inquiry as an orientation for learning, teaching and teacher education', in G. Wells and G. Claxton (eds) *Learning for Life in the 21st Century: sociocultural perspectives on the future of education*, Oxford: Blackwell.

Wells, G. (2002b) 'Dialogue about knowledge building', in B. Smith (ed.) *Liberal Education in a Knowledge Society*, La Salle, IL: Open Court.

Westheimer, J. (1998) *Among Schoolteachers: community, autonomy, and ideology in teachers' work*, New York: Teachers College Press.

Westheimer, J. (1999) 'Communities and consequences: an inquiry into ideology and practice in teachers' professional work', *Educational Administration Quarterly* 35, 1: 71–105.

Wiley, S.D. (2001) 'Contextual effects on student achievement: school leadership and professional community', *Journal of Educational Change* 2, 1: 1–33.

Williams, L. and Downing, J. (1998) 'Membership and belonging in inclusive classrooms: what do middle school students have to say?', *Journal of the Association for Persons with Severe Handicaps* 23, 2: 98–110.

Willms, J.D. (2003) *Student Engagement at School: a sense of belonging and participation. Results from PISA 2000*, Paris: Organisation for Economic Co-operation and Development.

Wrigley, T. (2000) 'Misunderstanding school improvement', *Improving Schools* 3, 1: 23–9.

Index